Great Conquerors

Other Books in the History Makers Series:

Great Conquerors

By Claire Price-Groff

Lucent Books
P.O. Box 289011, San Diego, CA 92198-9011

To Jenner, Ashleigh, Taylor, Kyle, and Kirsten.

Library of Congress Cataloging-in-Publication Data

Price-Groff, Claire.
    Great conquerors / by Claire Price-Groff.
        p.   cm. — (History makers)
    Includes bibliographical references (p.   ) and index.
    Contents: Two thousand years of conquerors—Alexander the Great—
Augustus the Great—Attila—Charlemagne—Genghis Kahn—Napoleon
Bonaparte.
    ISBN 1-56006-612-1 (lib. bdg. : alk. paper)
    1. Conquerors Biography Juvenile literature.   [1. Kings, queens,
rulers, etc.]   I. Title.   II. Series.
D107.P75   2000
920.02—dc21   99-41983
[B]   CIP

Cover photos: Center, Napoleon; clockwise from top right, Charlemagne,
Alexander the Great, Augustus

CONTENTS

FOREWORD

The literary form most often referred to as "multiple biography" was perfected in the first century A.D. by Plutarch, a perceptive and talented moralist and historian who hailed from the small town of Chaeronea in central Greece. His most famous work, *Parallel Lives*, consists of a long series of biographies of noteworthy ancient Greek and Roman statesmen and military leaders. Frequently, Plutarch compares a famous Greek to a famous Roman, pointing out similarities in personality and achievements. These expertly constructed and very readable tracts provided later historians and others, including playwrights like Shakespeare, with priceless information about prominent ancient personages and also inspired new generations of writers to tackle the multiple biography genre.

The Lucent History Makers series proudly carries on the venerable tradition handed down from Plutarch. Each volume in the series consists of a set of five to eight biographies of important and influential historical figures who were linked together by a common factor. In *Rulers of Ancient Rome*, for example, all the figures were generals, consuls, or emperors of either the Roman Republic or Empire; while the subjects of *Fighters Against American Slavery*, though they lived in different places and times, all shared the same goal, namely the eradication of human servitude. Mindful that politicians and military leaders are not (and never have been) the only people who shape the course of history, the editors of the series have also included representatives from a wide range of endeavors, including scientists, artists, writers, philosophers, religious leaders, and sports figures.

Each book is intended to give a range of figures—some well known, others less known; some who made a great impact on history, others who made only a small impact. For instance, by making Columbus's initial voyage possible, Spain's Queen Isabella I, featured in *Women Leaders of Nations*, helped to open up the New World to exploration and exploitation by the European powers. Unarguably, therefore, she made a major contribution to a series of events that had momentous consequences for the entire world. By contrast, Catherine II, the eighteenth-century Russian queen, and Golda Meir, the modern Israeli prime minister, did not play roles of global impact; however, their policies and actions significantly influenced the historical development of both their own countries and their regional neighbors. Regardless of their relative importance in the greater historical scheme, all of the figures chronicled in the History Makers series made contributions to posterity; and their public achievements, as well as what is known about their private lives, are presented and evaluated in light of the most recent scholarship.

In addition, each volume in the series is documented and substantiated by a wide array of primary and secondary source quotations. The primary source quotes enliven the text by presenting eyewitness views of the times and culture in which each history maker lived; while the secondary source quotes, taken from the works of respected modern scholars, offer expert elaboration and/ or critical commentary. Each quote is footnoted, demonstrating to the reader exactly where biographers find their information. The footnotes also provide the reader with the means of conducting additional research. Finally, to further guide and illuminate readers, each volume in the series features photographs, two bibliographies, and a comprehensive index.

The History Makers series provides both students engaged in research and more casual readers with informative, enlightening, and entertaining overviews of individuals from a variety of circumstances, professions, and backgrounds. No doubt all of them, whether loved or hated, benevolent or cruel, constructive or destructive, will remain endlessly fascinating to each new generation seeking to identify the forces that shaped their world.

CHAPTER 1

Two Thousand Years of Conquerors

Some historians argue that history is made by pivotal leaders whose actions shape both the times they live in and the future. Others feel that history is shaped by events and that leaders are merely reacting to those events. But regardless of historical theory, it is clear that the six conquerors profiled in this book have been pivotal in shaping history.

All conquerors become leaders, not through election or inheritance, but through the use of armed power. All conquerors possess not only ambition, but also foresight, intelligence, decisiveness—and often, ruthlessness and cruelty. Each of the men whose stories are told here had these qualities. But exercising military might is one thing. Governing a conquered territory is quite another, and it requires a different set of leadership qualities. Not all conquerors have been able to transform themselves from military leaders to effective rulers. These six conquerors stand out because they succeeded. Though these men could be cruel and despotic, once they had amassed their empires, they showed themselves to be able and, for the most part, wise and judicious administrators. They formulated equitable laws. They sponsored the building of roads and public works. They encouraged trade and economic growth.

Many of these men felt they had godlike qualities. Alexander proclaimed himself a god. Augustus, who publicly refrained from doing so, was deified after his death. Both Attila and Genghis Khan believed they had been chosen by their gods to rule the earth. Charlemagne, like a long series of European Christian kings after him, was crowned by the pope, signifying that his rule was in accordance with the will of God. In later years rulers extended the notion of divine approval by claiming to reign as a matter of God-given right. This idea of divine right was questioned by Napoleon's time, however. The French leader never claimed to be a god, nor did he claim any divine right to rule, though he once jokingly regetted that he could not do as Alexander had done, namely, proclaim himself a living god.

Each of these conquerors possessed a magnetic charisma that inspired intense loyalty in others. Alexander's men willingly walked miles through the desert to bring him water when he was ill. Napoleon's soldiers followed him to their deaths through the snows of a fierce Russian winter.

All except Alexander wanted to establish dynasties that would follow them. Most were not successful. Augustus was. He established an empire that lasted for several centuries.

Genghis Khan, Attila, and Charlemagne left their empires to their sons, but none was able to sustain the inheritance for long. However, one of Genghis Khan's grandsons, Kublai Khan, was himself a conqueror who founded the Mongol Yuan dynasty that ruled China for almost a hundred years.

Napoleon was the world's most profligate practitioner of nepotism, placing several members of his family in powerful positions and on various thrones of Europe. He tried desperately to establish a dynasty, but his empire collapsed with his final defeat at Waterloo.

Conquerors of the Ancient World

Alexander the Great was not the first conqueror of the ancient world—in fact, though we consider his world "ancient," thousands of years of history preceded him. He was, however, the first conqueror whose empire spanned both the east and west. Although Alexander inherited a kingdom from his father, it was his own indomitable ambition that led him to lay the foundation for an empire that spread Greek thought and culture to most of the known world. James Breasted, the noted historian, said:

> Although so short, his was without doubt the most influential and impressive individual life that the world had ever seen. Alexander's support of science and his persistent interest in it have led many governments ever since to realize that an enlightened government must support science. His campaigns and the cities he founded carried Greek civilization far into Asia and spread Greek art throughout India and China. World commerce was enormously increased by the removal of all national barriers. In statesmanship, Alexander's shadow, like that of some giant tree, fell far across Europe; and it is still there.[1]

Alexander the Great controlled a vast empire stretching from Greece to India.

During the centuries when the Hellenistic world was at its height, the Romans were growing ever stronger, until eventually, they established their own empire and replaced Greek culture with their own. Augustus the Great followed on the heels of several other Roman conquerors, but he was the one who transformed Rome from a small republic ruling over its provinces to a world empire administered by a strong central government. Unlike Alexander, whose empire did not outlast his own lifetime, the empire Augustus established lasted in the West for close to five hundred years and in the East for almost fifteen hundred years. During this long span of time, Roman culture and heritage was dispersed throughout much of Europe and the Middle East. David Stockton, in an essay included in *The Oxford History of the Classical World*, writes, "It was his achievement that . . . gave to the Roman world a freedom from war and fear of war unmatched in its duration, and that freedom under the law, one of the ideals of classical Greece and republican Rome, survived to be transmitted to modern Europe."[2]

Conquerors of the Medieval World

In the fourth and fifth centuries, the Germanic tribes living to the north of Italy made repeated raids across Roman borders. Among these invaders, Attila and his Huns were, for a brief time, preeminent. Attila, who conquered much of eastern and central Europe, was the most powerful non-Roman of his day and is even now considered to have been one of the world's most brilliant military leaders. But unlike Alexander and Augustus, who are remembered as heroes and role models, most of the Western world regards Attila as a brutal savage. Patrick Howarth, who has studied Attila extensively, explains why:

> The western world has gained its knowledge of the Huns from prejudiced and predominantly hostile sources. The earliest commentators were citizens of the Roman Empire,

who held the prevailing derogatory view of [Huns as] barbarians. They were succeeded by Christian chroniclers, who condemned the Huns as pagans and regarded Attila as an instrument sent by God to punish people for their sins.[3]

Though Attila's empire—as well as the Huns themselves—disappeared into obscurity soon after the leader's death, Attila was at least partly responsible for the collapse of the western portion of the Roman Empire and the end of the ancient world. Following Rome's collapse, Europe entered the Middle Ages and for several centuries was ruled by a number of Germanic chieftains, each of whom controlled his own domain. During this time, much of the technology introduced by the Romans fell into disuse, and illiteracy prevented most people from knowing anything of Roman and Greek science, philosophy, and literature.

It would not be until after the tenth or eleventh century that the legacies of the Hellenistic and Roman worlds would be permanently restored as the basis of European culture. However, in the late 700s

The Huns were one of the Germanic groups who seized control of the remnants of the Western Roman Empire. The Romans labeled the Huns barbarians and savages.

and early 800s during the reign of Charlemagne, there was a brief respite from this cultural darkness. Charlemagne, who amassed the greatest empire in Europe since Attila, was ahead of his time. Though like most conquerors he caused much destruction and death, he is remembered more for his endeavors to introduce technological innovations to his domain and for his patronage of learning and the arts. Charlemagne, or Charles, was revered in his own time, and after his death many legends grew up about him, as shown in this excerpt from the medieval epic poem, *Song of Roland*, which commemorates a terrible defeat suffered by his army.

> In Rouncesvalles Charles now has set his feet
> And for the dead he finds begins to weep. . . .
> He sees his nephew lying on the green grass.
> No wonder, then, that Charles is full of wrath.
> Dismounts and goes to him
> his heart is sad.
> He holds the count between his own two hands
> And on the body faints, so sharp's the pang.
> My friend Roland, God lay your soul on flowers
> In Paradise with all the glorious host.
> You came to Spain with a cruel overlord.
> No day shall pass henseforth that I'll not mourn.[4]

As for the legacy he left behind, one historian

> has compared the glory of Charlemagne to a brilliant meteor, rising suddenly out of the darkness of barbarism to disappear no less suddenly in the darkness of feudalism. But the light of this meteor was not extinguished, and reviving civilization owed much [to] the Great Emperor of the Franks. His ruling hand is seen in the legislation of his time, as well as in the administration of laws. He encouraged learning; he upheld the clergy, who were the only peaceful and intellectual class, against the encroaching and turbulent barons.[5]

By the middle of the twelfth century, Europe was at the height of the Middle Ages, that time of petty wars between small kingdoms, of fortresses and castles, and of knights and crusades. After Charlemagne, no single conqueror or leader dominated. In Asia, however, a strong conqueror did arise.

Genghis Khan, like Attila before him, came from a nomadic tribe out of the east. Genghis Khan's first accomplishment was to unite as the Mongolian people the various tribes from the steppes lying to the west and north of China. Then, he conquered China, a country with a civilization and culture even more ancient than that of Greece and Rome. Next, he turned to the west, and before he died had amassed an empire that extended from China to eastern Europe. Though much of his empire fell away after his death, Mongolia remained intact and was ruled by his successors for generations.

Europe experienced a revival of classical culture under Charlemagne, who promoted education and the arts.

Early Conquerors of the Modern World

Six hundred years after Genghis Khan ruled the East and almost a thousand years after Charlemagne ruled Europe, a new age dawned. The eighteenth century, sometimes referred to as the Age of Enlightenment or the Age of Reason, was a time of questioning the belief in the divine right of kings and monarchs. Philosophers such as Rousseau and Voltaire wrote of equality and promoted the idea of the ability of humans to determine their own destinies.

The revolt of the colonies in North America spurred similar revolts in Europe, the first of which occurred in France. But unlike the revolt in the colonies, the French Revolution spawned a long period of chaos and instability. Into this chaos came an insignificant young man with neither family connections nor money in back of him. Through cunning, chance, daring, and intelligence, Napoleon Bonaparte worked his way to the top, becoming ruler of France and then conqueror of much of Europe. Though he proclaimed democratic ideals, he instituted absolute tyranny. But the systems he established for administering the country and civil code, which bears his name, incorporated some of Rousseau's and Voltaire's ideals about equality and basic democratic principles. Napoleon was as able an administrator as he was a conqueror. Many of the structural changes he instituted in France remain in effect today.

Modern opinions on Napoleon are divided. Some historians feel the devastation he left in his wake and his assumption of total power outweigh any good he did. Eugene Tarlé says, "In all his political undertakings, Napoleon's ultimate purpose was to establish and consolidate his complete supremacy."[6] Edward Ashcroft, on the other hand, minimizes his negative aspects and praises him: "He is rightly called the Man of Destiny. . . . Unlike other dictators who have tried in vain to impose their wills on the world, his crimes never made him into a figure the world grew to hate."[7]

Although Napoleon was an absolute ruler, much of his legal code was based on democratic ideals. Some of his administration systems are still in use in France today.

Faded Empires, Enduring Legacies

Though their empires may have faded, the legacies these men left behind have not. Much of today's culture, both in the West and in the East, has been shaped by these six men. The principles of Greek-style architecture and art are still used today. Many of our laws and governmental structures are derived from Roman forms. Attila profoundly changed methods of warfare. If it were not for Charlemagne, western Europe might not have become as solidly Christianized as it did. Genghis Khan united the Mongol people, bringing many important changes to Asia, and many of Napoleon's modifications of the structure of French government remain in place today.

CHAPTER 2

Alexander the Great: Founder of the Hellenistic Age

On her wedding night, Alexander's mother, Olympias, dreamed that her womb was struck by lightning, which ignited a great sheet of fire around her body but did not consume her. She was sure this meant that she was carrying a child fathered by a god. Alexander's father, Philip, dreamed that he had sealed his wife's womb with an image of a lion. Soothsayers predicted the child would be both bold and invincible.

Olympias, princess of the small kingdom of Epirus, and Philip, who would become king of Macedon, named their son Alexander.

Hercules, the mythological Greek hero from whom King Philip believed he was descended.

It was not only the strange dreams of his conception that foretold greatness for this child, but his ancestry as well. His mother claimed descent from Achilles, the legendary hero of the Trojan War, immortalized by the poet Homer in his epic, the *Iliad*. And Philip claimed an ancestor perhaps even more exalted—none other than Hercules, a son of Zeus, the king of all the Greek gods. Both Achilles and Hercules were mortals who attained the status of gods after their deaths. Growing up with the soothsayers' prophecies for him and with stories about his illustrious ancestry, Alexander knew one thing for certain: he would be a great man.

In a mere eleven years, Alexander built an empire that encompassed all of Greece, the Middle East, central Asia, and part of

India, launching what historians call the Hellenistic Age. In this period, which lasted for over two centuries, Greek literature, art, architecture, language, and thought dominated the civilized world. Indeed, Hellenistic culture would become the foundation of Rome and all of Western civilization. According to historian James Breasted, "In a word, the brief life of Alexander the Great completely transformed the world."[8]

Alexander was born in Pella, the ancient capital of Macedonia, a small kingdom to the north of Greece, on July 20, 356 B.C. Greece was not a monarchy. It was not even a single nation, but a collection of individual city-states, each with its own form of government. Though individuals were loyal to their city-states, all the people of Greece thought of themselves as Greek. And though they spoke the same language and worshiped the same gods as the people of Macedon, the Greeks were quite different from the Macedonians.

Macedonians lived in a tribal culture made up of farmers and herders. They were not as cosmopolitan as their Greek neighbors, who lived in cities and pursued careers in philosophy, architecture, medicine, and literature. Greeks had long ago discarded kings and tyrants as their rulers; instead, the people met in assemblies to choose their leaders and laws. While most Macedonians considered themselves part of the Greek peoples, most Greeks considered Macedonians to be uncultured barbarians.

By the time Alexander was sixteen, his father, Philip II, had become king of Macedonia. Philip, long an admirer of Greek civilization, wanted to bring the Greek city-states under his control. During his reign, Philip would build a strong army and conquer the Greek colonies on the coast of Macedonia and Thrace, thus uniting all Greek city-states under his leadership. Philip's empire and the army he built to defend it would pave the way for Alexander to build his own, far greater empire.

Along with military and political power, Alexander inherited his father's ambition and, according to Plutarch, a Greek biographer who lived from around A.D. 46 to 120, "Each time he heard of another of his father's victories, he said to his friends, 'Boys, my father will forestall me in everything. There will be nothing great or spectacular for you and me to show the world.'"[9]

Early Years and Education

Knowing he was training a future king, Philip made sure his son had the finest tutors available. One of his early tutors was Leonidas, an uncle of Olympias, who trained Alexander in physical endurance, horsemanship, and archery as well as in the basics of arithmetic and reading. Another early tutor, Lysimachus, invented a game in which Alexander acted out the part of his hero Achilles. Following on Olympias's claim of ancestry to this hero of heroes, the play-acting provided Alexander with a perfect role model. Jack Balcer, in an essay on Alexander, says that "[in] Alexander's youthful mind, Achilles became the epitome [embodiment] of the aristocratic warrior."[10]

When Alexander was thirteen, Philip told him he wanted him to study philosophy, "so that," he said, "you may not do a great many things of the sort that I am sorry to have done."[11] Philip persuaded Aristotle, one of Greece's greatest philosophers and thinkers, to accept his son as a pupil. Aristotle instructed Alexander and a few of his close friends in philosophy, government, politics, poetry, drama, and the sciences. It was under Aristotle's teaching that Alexander studied the classics of Greek literature, especially the *Iliad,* featuring his hero Achilles. Alexander so loved Homer's long poem that Aristotle prepared a special annotated edition of it for him, which Alexander forever after carried with him, often sleeping with it under his pillow. In Breasted's view,

A medieval manuscript illumination shows Aristotle tutoring Alexander. Aristotle exposed the young prince's mind to philosophy, science, and poetry, among other subjects.

18

"The deeds of the ancient heroes touched and kindled his [Alexander's] youthful imagination and lent a heroic tinge to his whole character."[12]

Aristotle also taught Alexander botany, zoology, and medicine, and Alexander put all this knowledge to use during his military campaigns. As a general, he collected specimens of plants and animals to study and tended his soldiers' illnesses and wounds.

Alexander seems to have loved Aristotle as much as he did his father. "The one had given me life, but the Philosopher [Aristotle] had shown me how to live well,"[13] he reportedly said. It was probably under Aristotle's influence that Alexander formulated his thoughts on how to conduct himself as a soldier and leader.

It is no wonder that Alexander, having always been taught that he was destined for greatness, exhibited extraordinary self-confidence even as a youth. When he was around thirteen, someone offered to sell Philip a horse named Bucephalus. The horse was not young and had probably already been trained for fighting, but none of Philip's grooms was able to mount the animal. Philip said the horse was useless and ordered it taken away. But Alexander disagreed. "What a magnificent horse they are losing, and all because they don't know how to handle him, or dare not try!" he said.

Philip scolded his son. "Are you finding fault with your elders because you think you can manage a horse better?"

"At least I could manage this one better,"[14] said Alexander.

Alexander, who had noticed that the animal shied and reared at shadows, offered to pay the whole price of the horse if he were unable to tame him.

Positioning himself so that no shadow lay between himself and Bucephalus, Alexander spoke to the horse to calm him, then mounted and rode away. At this Philip said, "My boy, you must find a kingdom big enough for your ambitions. Macedonia is too little for you."[15] Bucephalus became Alexander's favorite steed.

Alexander's childhood ended at sixteen, when his father, busy with an expedition to Byzantium, left the youth in charge of Macedonia. Plutarch says that during this time, "He [Alexander] defeated the Maedi [a tribe in northeastern Macedonia] who had risen in revolt, captured their city, drove out its barbarous inhabitants, established a colony of Greeks assembled from various regions, and named it Alexandroupolis."[16]

Later that same year, Alexander joined his father in a battle against Thebes and Athens, two of the strongest city-states. The battle took place at Chaeronea, where Alexander headed a section of cavalry and led an assault against the Sacred Band, the best

Alexander tames Bucephalus, the horse deemed unmanageable by Philip and his groomsmen.

soldiers of Thebes. It was this battle which made Philip the undisputed ruler of Greece, and Alexander played a significant part in this victory. Plutarch says, "nothing pleased him [Philip] more than to hear his subjects call himself their general and Alexander their king."[17]

At this time, Philip called a meeting of the city-states and re-established the ancient Corinthian League, a body made up of representatives from each state. At the meeting, when he announced his plans to invade Persia, an old enemy of both Greece and Macedon, the league elected him commander in chief of all Greek forces. Philip was proud of his son's bravery and leadership in this battle and counted him a valuable asset in the coming war.

Alexander and Philip may have had respect and admiration for each other on the battlefield, but this was not so in their private life. When Alexander was nineteen, Philip divorced Olympias and married Cleopatra, the daughter of a Macedonian nobleman (not the Egyptian Cleopatra, who lived much later). Olympias convinced Alexander that the new marriage threatened his position as Philip's heir: since Cleopatra was Macedonian while Olympias was not, if Cleopatra had a son, he would have stronger claims on the Macedonian throne than Alexander. At his father's wedding, Alexander became angry when a Macedonian general toasted the new bride, saying he hoped the gods would give her a son that would be a more legitimate heir to the throne than Alexander. Plutarch wrote:

> Alexander flew into rage at these words, shouted at him, "Villain, do you take me for a bastard then?" and hurled a drinking-cup at his head. At this Philip lurched to his feet, drew his sword against his son, but fortunately for them both he was so overcome with drink and rage that he tripped and fell headlong. Alexander jeered at him and

cried out, "Here is the man who was making ready to cross from Europe to Asia, and who cannot even cross from one table to another without losing his balance."[18]

Alexander then left to live in neighboring Illyria. Father and son remained estranged for several months until a friend convinced Philip to reconcile with Alexander, which he did. However, father and son retained bitter feelings for one another.

A Young King

The following year Philip had much to celebrate. His new wife had given birth to a son, his troops were preparing to invade Persia, and his daughter, Alexander's younger sister, was getting married. But his good fortune was short-lived. During the wedding festivities, Philip was assassinated by one of his bodyguards.

The assassin was caught and killed before anyone could question him. He was said to have been angry because he had been passed over for promotions, but it was known he was part of a conspiracy, and rumors hinted that Olympias might have been involved.

Alexander found and executed the other conspirators involved in his father's murder. Some ancient historians contend that after

At his daughter's wedding party, one of Philip's guards turns on the king and attacks him. Philip's assassination made the young Alexander king of Macedonia.

Philip's death, Olympias helped Alexander eliminate a possible future threat to his rule by killing Cleopatra and her young son. Some reports say the former queen had both her rival and the baby "roasted over a brazier,"[19] while others say she had the boy killed and then Cleopatra, grief-stricken, committed suicide. Plutarch says that Alexander was angry with his mother's gruesome meddling.

Alexander, now king, appealed to members of the Corinthian League to remain intact and to affirm their support of him. They did, but many in Greece still resented the idea of being ruled by a Macedonian and felt that because Alexander was young and inexperienced, they could easily rid themselves of him. Alexander wasted no time in dealing with these situations. When a rebellion began in Illyria, he marched north to quell it. From there, he went west to quiet uprisings along the banks of the Danube River.

When a rumor that Alexander had been killed in Illyria sparked a revolt in Thebes, the king brought his army to the gates of the city and demanded the surrender of its leaders. Alexander became so enraged at the Thebans' refusal to give up their chief citizens that he attacked the city with ferocity, allowing his soldiers to loot and pillage the homes, and burn the city to the ground. Historians tell us that over six thousand people were slain that day and that over thirty thousand were sold into slavery. But according to Mary Renault, Alexander personally saved a chosen few: "Priests, old guest-friends of Macedonians . . . and the descendants of Pindar [a Greek poet who lived from 518 to 438 B.C.], along with the poet's house."[20]

Alexander also spared the life of a woman who admitted killing a Macedonian soldier. The woman told Alexander that the soldier had raped her and demanded all her silver and gold. She told the soldier her treasure was hidden in her well and brought him to it, then, as he peered over the rim, she pushed him in and threw stones on top of him. Proudly, she also told Alexander that she was the daughter of the general who had led the Thebans against Philip at Chaeronea. Alexander was so impressed by the woman's boldness that he allowed her and her children to go free.

As to the brutality with which he treated Thebes, Plutarch says, "Certain it is, too, that in after-time he often repented of his severity to the Thebans, and his remorse had such influence on his temper as to make him ever after less rigorous to all others."[21] If the harshness with Thebes was intended to show that Alexander would not tolerate opposition, the ploy worked. The Athenians quickly surrendered to the young king.

Alexander rides through Thebes as his troops sack the city in 335 B.C., crushing the Thebans' revolt.

Alexander wanted to establish his leadership in Greece so he would be free to pursue his real dream—invading and conquering Persia. Like his father, Philip, Alexander believed that this act would exact revenge for Persia's invasion of Greece 150 years before. And it is also likely that Alexander wanted to conquer Persia to make his own mark on history. For although today the descendants of the ancient Persians live mainly in the relatively small country of Iran, in Alexander's time, the Persian Empire, ruled by Darius III, extended from modern-day Turkey well into central Asia, an area as large as the continental United States.

Like most people of his time, Alexander sought divine guidance in important undertakings, appealing to the gods through the intercession

Alexander consults with the oracle of Delphi before his invasion of Persia.

of priests or priestesses known as oracles. Before setting out on his first campaign against Persia, he consulted the oracle at the shrine of Apollo at Delphi. The priestess, presumably speaking for the god himself, said, "My son, thou art invincible."[22] Alexander believed her.

Conquering Persia

In the spring of 334 B.C., Alexander crossed the narrow body of water called the Hellespont, which separated Greece from Persia. To ready himself for the coming battles, he stopped at Troy to visit the grave of Achilles. Paying homage to the ancient hero in a traditional custom, Alexander stripped naked and ran around the grave, then placed a wreath on it. He also "made a gift of his armor to the temple, and took in exchange, from where they hung on temple walls, some weapons which were still preserved from the Trojan War."[23] Feeling as strongly as he did about Greek history, and his own place in it, this was probably one of the most important moments in Alexander's life.

His first confrontation with the Persian army was at Granicus (now Kocabas, in Turkey). Alexander knew he was outnumbered, but he had faith in his men, whom he motivated by reciting stirring passages from the *Iliad*.

Alexander was victorious, and after the battle, he sent a tribute of booty and arms to Athens as an offering to Athena, the goddess of war, with a letter saying, "Alexander the son of Philip, and the Grecians, except the Lacedaemonians (Spartans), won these from the barbarians who inhabit Asia."[24] His motive in doing this was to show the Athenians that it was in their interest to give him their support.

From Granicus, Alexander marched into the interior of Asia Minor, where most cities welcomed him as a liberator, come to free them from their Persian rulers. Most of these cities were former Greek city-states that had been conquered by Persia. One mark of Alexander's brilliance was that unlike many generals, he allowed those he conquered to keep their own religions and customs. But more than that, he acknowledged the local gods and paid tribute to them. He also replaced Persian autocratic rule with a more democratic one overseen by local governors or satraps; the army, however, remained strictly in Macedonian hands.

At Issus in the northeastern part of present-day Syria, Alexander was again victorious despite being outnumbered by Darius's army. In fact, he beat the Persians so badly that Darius fled for his life, leaving behind his mother, his wife, and three young daughters. In the aftermath of this battle, Alexander said, "Let us now cleanse ourselves from the toils of war in the bath of Darius." When Alexander saw the splendor of the Asian monarch's bathing facilities, he said, "This, it seems is royalty."[25]

Later, Alexander learned that Darius's wife, children, and mother were among the women wandering the camp wondering what their fate would be. He guaranteed the royal family their safety and assured them that they would be allowed to keep their possessions. They traveled with Alexander's army, and Alexander became good friends with Darius's mother. In his determination to be a fair and just ruler, when he heard that two of his soldiers had abused women prisoners, he demanded an investigation and ordered that if found guilty, the culprits be executed "as wild beasts."

In response to his defeat at Issus, Darius wrote Alexander, offering him money, the hand of one of his daughters, and all the lands east of the Euphrates in exchange for peace. Alexander's general, Parmenio, said, "I would accept, were I Alexander," and Alexander replied, "I, too, were I Parmenio!"[26] But being Alexander, he refused.

From Issus, Alexander headed south along the eastern Mediterranean coast of the Persian Empire, taking most cities with ease. But not all cities gladly opened their gates to him. The Phoenician port of Tyre, which was partly on the mainland and partly an island, fled to the island rather than surrender. Alexander destroyed the mainland portion of the city and held the island under siege for seven months while he used rubble from the city to build a causeway to the island. While he showed leniency, generosity, and

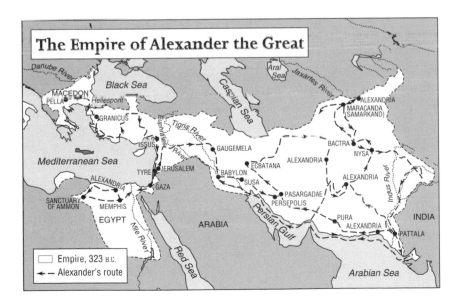

The Empire of Alexander the Great

Danube River, Black Sea, MACEDON, PELLA, Hellespont, GRANICUS, Aral Sea, Jaxartes River, Caspian Sea, Tigris River, ISSUS, Euphrates River, ALEXANDRIA, MARACANDA (SAMARKAND), Mediterranean Sea, GAUGEMELA, BACTRA, NYSA, TYRE, JERUSALEM, BABYLON, ECBATANA, ALEXANDRIA, ALEXANDRIA, ALEXANDRIA, GAZA, SUSA, Indus River, SANCTUARY OF AMMON, MEMPHIS, PASARGADAE, PERSEPOLIS, PURA, ALEXANDRIA, INDIA, EGYPT, Nile River, ARABIA, Persian Gulf, PATTALA

Empire, 323 B.C.
← Alexander's route

Red Sea, Arabian Sea

kindness to the cities that accepted him without a fight, he treated Tyre as he had Thebes, burning the city and selling the people into slavery.

The Egyptian Oracle

Next, Alexander marched south and west into Egypt, gaining control of the entire eastern Mediterranean. Again most cities welcomed him as a liberator, some because they did not want their cities sacked as Tyre had been, and others because they were glad to be freed of Persian domination. Not only did the Egyptians welcome Alexander's arrival, they crowned him a pharaoh, an honor that was accompanied by an even higher status: that of a living god.

The Egyptians welcomed Alexander, crowned him pharaoh, and considered him a divine ruler.

While in Egypt, Alexander took a strange detour, traveling three hundred miles out of his way through the desert to consult the oracle of Ammon-Zeus at Siwa. The god Ammon was to the Egyptians what Apollo was to the Greeks. Both were supposed to be sons of Zeus, the highest god.

No one knows why Alexander made this journey. Perhaps he was thinking of his familial connections to Hercules and Achilles, both said to be descendants of Zeus, which would have made him related to Ammon. Perhaps he was repeating a legendary journey of Hercules to visit the same oracle. Perhaps he was seeking confirmation of his mother's intimations that he had been fathered by a god.

At any rate, when he arrived at the oracle, he was greeted with enthusiasm by the priestess, who acknowledged him as the son of Ammon and granted him a private audience. Alexander never told anyone what was discussed. "His sole comment," says Mary Renault, "was that he had had the answer his soul desired."[27] Most historians believe that he was told he truly was a descendant of Zeus, a son of Ammon, and destined to rule over all humankind.

From that time on, he sat on a golden throne, wore sacred vestments, and adorned his head with a crown of two rams' horns similar to the one worn by the statue of Ammon. And in 324 B.C. he sent word to all Greek states except Macedonia that he was to be recognized as a son of Ammon-Zeus. However, he was well aware of his less than godly nature. Once, when injured by an arrow he said, "This, you see, is blood, and not such ichor [the fluid said to take the place of blood in the mythical Greek gods] as flows from the wounds of the immortals."[28]

He later claimed the oracle had revealed that his true mission was to unite Europe, Asia, and North Africa into a world brotherhood sharing social, cultural, ethnic, and political goals. To bring about this mission, he encouraged citizens from all parts of his growing empire to settle in the seventy cities he founded, many of which he named Alexandria. He personally marked out the borders and planned the design for the Alexandria in Egypt, which became a center of learning that flourished for centuries. Along with his army, Alexander brought scientists and men of learning to fully explore conquered lands. According to James Breasted, "He was as much interested in science as he was in conquests, and his great campaign became the first scientific expedition in history."[29]

World Conqueror

Upon completing his conquest of Egypt, Alexander headed back to Phoenecia. En route, he engaged Darius at Gaugemela, where once again the Persian fled. This was Alexander's final major victory.

Alexander was now master of the Persian Empire. He had first marched through Babylon on his way east. Now, he returned to Babylon "as King of Babylon, in a state chariot plated with gold, among splendours never to be surpassed in the triumphs of the Caesars,"[30] and an inscription on the island of Rhodes from the year 330 B.C. honored him as "lord of Asia." From Babylon, he proceeded to Susa, a city near the Persian Gulf, where he left Darius's family and claimed the spoils of the former king's treasury.

While not on the battlefield, Alexander began his day with a tribute to the gods. If he had no pressing military matters to attend to, he often slept late, went hunting, wrote his memoirs, or read. He dined late and enjoyed leisurely conversation over a glass of wine. According to Plutarch, his tastes in eating were plain. "When any rare fish or fruits were sent him, he would distribute them among his friends, and often reserve nothing for himself."[31]

During one respite between battles, he decided to find and kill Darius. When he reached Darius's camp, however, he found a chaotic situation, with Darius dying, having been mortally wounded by Bessus, a Persian general. In a show of respect, Alexander covered his enemy's body with his own cloak. He then sent the remains to Darius's mother for proper burial.

Darius, king of Persia, was killed by one of his own generals.

Later, Bessus headed a revolt in the eastern provinces. Alexander hunted him down and, in the Persian manner, had him flogged, then cut off his ears and nose. That punishment was for the revolt. But for murdering Darius, Alexander had Bessus bound by his arms and legs to two trees which had been tied together, then allowed to spring apart, tearing Bessus's body to pieces.

Sometime after the death of Darius, Alexander began dressing in the Persian style, surrounding himself with luxurious furnishings, and demanding that underlings prostrate themselves before him. "At every new remove from Greece, Alexander was becoming less and less a Greek, more and more a barbarian king,"[32] wrote Will Durant.

As part of his hopes of merging Greek and Persian cultures, he married Roxana, a Persian princess, and later took two more Persian wives. He also offered gifts and special incentives to his officers if they married Persian women, and a great many of them did so. He appointed many Persians to high positions and trained thousands of Persian youths, whom he welcomed into his armed forces.

Not content with Persia and Egypt, Alexander pushed his army into India, crossing the Indus River and the Punjab. At the Hyphasis River, he engaged Porus, one of India's most powerful kings, and defeated him in battle. During this campaign, Alexander's horse Bucephalus died. As testament to the steed's many years of faithfulness, Alexander named a city after him.

Alexander was determined to reach the Ganges River, but his men were tired of fighting far from home and refused to go farther. Alexander sent some of the men home, but convinced others to stay to build a fleet of eight hundred ships to explore the Indus and sail back to the Persian Gulf. While camped at the Hyphasis, he built altars to the twelve gods of Olympus. Part of his army then sailed home, and Alexander led the rest back toward Babylon in a grueling march during which many died from thirst, heat, and disease. As he approached close to Babylon, he stopped at Opis, where he made an oath to the peoples he had conquered, in which he said, in part:

> I wish all of you . . . to live happily, in peace. All mortals from now on will live like one people, united, and peacefully working towards a common prosperity. . . . I am not interested in the origin or race of citizens. I only distinguish them on the basis of their virtue.[33]

By now, Alexander had conquered most of the world known to his people. He had founded great cities and monuments. He introduced many innovations to Greek life and spread Greek learning and culture throughout his domains. Yet he had further ambitions. He wanted to explore and sail completely around the Arabian peninsula. He wanted to extend his conquests to the Western world, and to do this, he planned to build a fleet of a thousand battleships and a great highway along the northern coast of Africa.

In the spring of 323 B.C., he returned to Babylon and, shortly after his arrival, contracted a fever and died at the age of thirty-three. Many ancient and modern historians have suggested that he might have been poisoned, but this has never been proven.

In less than thirteen years, Alexander had become ruler of much of the world. Most ancient Greek texts contend that his body was taken to Alexandria, Egypt, where it was placed in a golden cof-

The Indian king Porus surrenders to Alexander in 326 B.C.

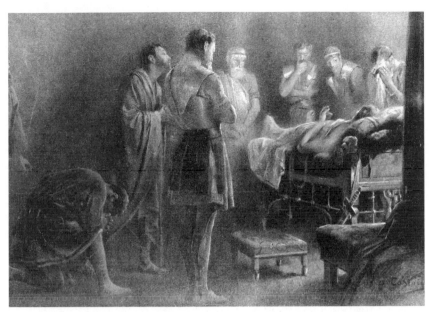

When asked to whom he would leave his empire, the dying Alexander supposedly replied, "To the strongest."

fin. One tradition has it that shortly before he died, he was asked whom he had chosen as his successor. According to Arrian, a later Greek historian, he said, "'Hoti to Kratisto'—'to the strongest.'"[34] His answer led to quarrels among his generals, and it was not long before the empire was divided among them.

But the Hellenistic culture he had spread remained dominant for hundreds of years until the territories he had conquered were taken over by the Romans, who considered Alexander to be one of the greatest of Greek warriors. Indeed, it was the Romans who bestowed on Alexander the epithet, the Great.

Where Is Alexander Today?

Alexander made the news in 1995 when Liand Souvaltzi, a Greek archaeologist, claimed to have found his tomb, not in Alexandria, but near Siwa, where he had first been proclaimed a god. Souvaltzi says the site is adorned with Macedonian oak-leaf designs and that records show that Alexander had requested his burial to be at Siwa. She also claims to have found a stone inscribed with Alexander's personal emblem—a star with eight rays.

Though many historians dispute her claim, Souvaltzi cites stone tablets with inscriptions that "prove" this to be Alexander's final resting place. This is a controversy not yet resolved. It remains one of many mysteries from a long past age.

CHAPTER 3

Augustus the Great: First Roman Emperor

He was short, slight of build, frail, and prone to illness. He was not a good athlete, nor was he a particularly good or brave soldier. In fact, he hated war and despised physical combat. Augustus the Great was far from the "ideal" example of a Roman warrior, and an unlikely conqueror. Yet he wrested power from men far older, stronger, and more experienced than he to become the first emperor of the Roman world.

Nicolaus of Damascus, an ancient historian and a contemporary of Augustus, wrote:

> For this man, having attained preeminent power and discretion, ruled over the greatest number of people within the memory of man, established the farthest boundaries for the Roman Empire, and settled securely not only the tribes of the Greeks and barbarians, but also their dispositions; at first with arms but afterward even without arms, by attracting them of their own free will.[35]

Michael Grant, one of today's leading authorities on the ancient world, evaluates Augustus this way: "Augustus was one of the most talented, energetic and skillful administrators that the world has ever known. The enormously far-reaching work of reorganization and rehabilitation which he undertook in every branch of his vast Empire created a new Roman Peace."[36]

Protégé of Caesar

Augustus was born in Rome as Gaius Octavian on September 23, 63 B.C. His mother, Atia, was Julius Caesar's niece, making Octavian the great man's grand-nephew. His father, also Gaius Octavian, came from a more humble background but had risen to the position of senator. Octavian was only four years old when his father died, but he became very close to his stepfather, Marcus Phillipus.

Though he was frail and suffered from asthma, Octavian was intelligent and well liked, a good-looking child with bright eyes and curly blond hair. Nicolaus observed that "Octavius [Roman spelling], at the age of about nine years, was an object of no little admiration to the Romans, exhibiting as he did great excellence of nature, young though he was; for he gave an oration before a large crowd and received much applause from grown men."[37] Nicolaus may have exaggerated the age at which this oration was given, but it is known that when he was twelve, Octavian presented the eulogy at the funeral of his grandmother Julia (Caesar's sister).

When Octavian was three years old, Julius Caesar, Pompey (another strong general), and Crassus (one of Rome's wealthiest citizens) formed the First Triumvirate, which then ruled all of Rome. Caesar was elected consul, the highest political position in Rome. He also appointed himself governor of Gaul, Rome's largest province, a region now occupied by Belgium and France. Thus as Octavian grew up, he watched his uncle become the most powerful man in Rome.

By the time Octavian was thirteen, Crassus had died and Pompey and many others had become afraid of Caesar's ever increasing ambition for power. A vicious civil war erupted, which eventually Caesar won when he defeated Pompey at Pharsala in 48 B.C. Caesar then became sole ruler of Rome in everything but title, which remained consul.

When Octavian was fifteen, Caesar introduced him into Roman politics in a traditional

After the chaos of the Roman civil wars, Augustus took control of the empire and led it into an era of peace and productivity.

ceremony that made Octavian an official member of Rome's ruling class. The youth was also elected to the college of pontifices, an honorary religious office. These ceremonies marked him as an adult, but Nicolaus points out that "though he was registered as of age according to law, his mother would not let him leave the house other than as he did before, when he was a child."[38]

Caesar invited Octavian to accompany him on his next military campaign in Africa, but Atia said he was too young and too frail for such a venture. However, when Caesar returned to Rome, he included Octavian in the victory celebrations just as if the boy had taken part in the war.

Julius Caesar, Octavian's uncle and later adoptive father.

The following year, Octavian's mother gave him permission to accompany Caesar on the campaign to conquer Spain. When the time came to leave, Octavian was sick in bed, but as soon as he recovered he left to join his uncle on what turned out to be a perilous journey. The contemporary Roman biographer Suetonius wrote that Octavian set out "with a very small escort, along roads held by the enemy, after a shipwreck, too, and in a state of semi-convalescence from a serious illness."[39]

Continuing to groom Octavian for a position of leadership, Caesar sent him to Apollonia on the west coast of Greece to complete his academic studies and receive military training.

A Rising Star

While in Apollonia, Octavian received a letter from his mother with the news that Julius Caesar had been assassinated by men who had been close to him, including Marcus Junius Brutus and Gaius Cassius Longinus. While some Romans applauded the assassins because they feared that Caesar had grown too powerful, others were angry and wanted to kill Caesar's murderers.

Atia urged Octavian to return to Rome at once to stake his claim as Caesar's possible successor. In the same mail packet he received a letter from his stepfather cautioning him that because he was related to Caesar, his life might be in danger and advising him to stay away from Rome. Octavian's friend Agrippa suggested that Octavian immediately take charge of Caesar's six legions and lead them to Rome to avenge Caesar's death.

But Octavian did not take anyone's advice. Instead he and Agrippa sailed to a small village on the west coast of Italy, carefully avoiding the larger port of Brundisium where Caesar's enemies might be watching for him. Then he slowly built a following by seeking out men who had fought for and supported Caesar. As James Breasted, author of the classic history, *The Conquest of Civilization*, observes, "This statesmanlike decision of character reveals the quality of the young man as he showed it both then and for years to follow."[40]

Octavian learned that Marc Antony, one of Caesar's top military advisers, had assumed leadership of the Senate and that the conspirators had fled to Greece. He also learned that Caesar's will made it clear that he had formally adopted Octavian as his son and heir, both to his vast fortune and to his place as ruler of the Roman people. Octavian demonstrated his political astuteness in immediately assuming Caesar's name, calling himself Gaius Julius Caesar. A modern historian, Henry Rowell, says of this move, "In one bold stroke, [Octavian] had created for himself a reservoir of power. He had made himself the person around whom all those who were loyal to Caesar's memory and incensed by his unworthy end could rally."[41]

Though word of Octavian's activities had reached Rome, Antony failed to take seriously this threat to his own grab for power. Cicero, one of Rome's leading citizens, however, was more perceptive. Cicero had been involved in the plot against Caesar because he opposed the idea of a dictatorship; rather, he wanted Rome to retain a more democratic government ruled by the Senate. In a letter to one of his friends, Cicero wrote, "His people address him as Caesar, but Phillippus [Octavian's stepfather] does not, and so I do not either. I hold that it is impossible for a loyal citizen to do so. We are surrounded by so many who threaten death to our friends. What do you think will happen when this boy comes to Rome? Unless I am much mistaken, [we] shall be crushed."[42]

When he arrived in Rome, Octavian learned that Marc Antony

Statesman and orator Cicero was one of the last supporters of the dying Republic.

not only was leading the movement against the conspirators but had been named as consul and furthermore had illegally seized a large portion of Caesar's wealth. Octavian knew that both Antony and Cicero would be formidable opponents to his plan to follow in his uncle's footsteps.

Politically astute despite his young age, Octavian realized that if he were to replace Caesar, he would have to first win the love and support of the people. Thus, playing to the Romans' great love of public entertainments, he put on, at his own expense, a series of elaborate games in Caesar's honor. In his speeches, he always referred to Caesar as "my father," which further endeared him to the people. Such tactics had the desired effect, and soon Octavian had the backing of the Senate and of most Roman citizens.

Then, with the army he had assembled, Octavian forced Antony to flee, first to northern Italy, and then to Gaul. In 43 B.C., before he agreed to engage in an all-out war against Antony, the twenty-year-old Octavian appeared before the Senate and demanded that the legislators elect him consul. The traditional minimum age for becoming consul was forty-three. According to Suetonius's account, "When the Senate hesitated to obey [vote to make Octavian consul], Cornelius, a centurion leading his deputation, opened his military cloak, displayed the hilt of his sword, and boldly said, 'If you do not make him Consul, this will!'"[43] Consuls were usually elected for one-year terms. Before the end of his life, Octavian would hold the consulship thirteen times, though not consecutively.

The Second Triumvirate

Octavian knew that he and his newly acquired small army stood little chance of defeating Antony, an experienced general with a large army. Octavian decided not to fight Antony. Instead, he once again demonstrated his shrewdness by making an alliance with Marcus Lepidus, another powerful general. Then, he and Lepidus met with Antony and proposed a joint rule of Rome and her provinces. The three leaders agreed to divide the empire, with Antony taking Egypt, not a Roman province, but a conquered territory; Lepidus taking North Africa; and Octavian taking Rome and all the western provinces. They called their partnership the Second Triumvirate, and the Senate granted them emergency powers to last for five years. Michael Grant describes the new triumvirate as "a dictatorial committee appointed by due process of law to reform the state and avenge Caesar's murder."[44]

The first move of the triumvirate was to proscribe certain individuals, formally naming them as enemies of the state and condemning them to death. The names of 120 senators and close to 2,000 others who opposed the Second Triumvirate were posted in a public square. Many of those proscribed fled Rome, leaving their money and property behind; hundreds who remained, including Cicero, were brutally murdered. All property and money of the proscribed individuals, whether living or dead, were confiscated to finance the triumvirate's planned war against Brutus and Cassius, two of the principal conspirator-assassins.

In agreeing to the proscriptions, Octavian showed himself to be not only an astute politician, but a power seeker capable of ruthlessness and cruelty as well. Breasted said of this period of Octavian's life, "Then playing the game of politics, with military power at his back and none too scrupulous a conscience, he showed himself a statesman no longer to be ignored."[45]

In October 42 B.C., the triumvirate's armies, led by Antony and Lepidus, defeated Brutus and Cassius in one of antiquity's most famous battles, at Phillipi in Macedonia. Brutus and Cassius were so humiliated by the defeat that they committed suicide.

During the battle, Octavian remained in his tent. He said he was sick and that his doctor had ordered him to stay out of the actual fighting. Many historians have wondered whether the true reason was fear. This may indeed have been the case, but in the years to come, Octavian would overcome his reluctance to fight and take part in many battles.

After Phillipi, Antony returned to Egypt, where he had formed an alliance with Queen Cleopatra, the last descendant of the Ptolemaic dynasty established hundreds of years earlier in the wake of Alexander the Great's conquest of that ancient land.

Eliminating Rivals

Over the next several years, Octavian faced many problems but managed to solve most of them through a combination of decisive actions and cunning political maneuvering. In an attempt to ease relations with Sextus Pompius, a political rival who controlled the island of Sicily, he married the man's daughter, Scribonia. However, within a few years, the rivalry between himself and Sextus escalated into war. And although the marriage to Scribonia produced Octavian's only living child, his daughter Julia, the marriage ended in divorce when Octavian fell in love with another woman. The other woman, Livia, however, was married, had one child, and was pregnant with her second. Since only a man could obtain a divorce, Octavian forced Livia's husband to divorce her. Octavian and Livia then married and remained so until Octavian died; he raised her two sons, Tiberius and Drusus.

Octavian was victorious in his war against Sextus on Sicily, but only through the help of his friend Agrippa, who had become one of his top aides and generals, and his fellow triumvir Lepidus. Agrippa attacked from the sea and Lepidus from Africa; Octavian was to attack from Italy. The campaigns of Agrippa and Lepidus proceeded as planned, but Octavian and half his squadron were shipwrecked in a storm. Upon landing on Sicily, he was surrounded by enemy cavalry and barely escaped. Once again, the battles took place without his participation.

Antony greets Cleopatra, queen of Egypt. Antony became romantically involved with Cleopatra and adopted many Egyptian customs and styles, which alienated him from the fiercely patriotic Romans.

As reward for his part in this war, Lepidus demanded Sicily, but Octavian considered the request an act against Rome. He also decided that it was time to eliminate Lepidus from the triumvirate. He persuaded the older general's troops to abandon him and allowed the disgraced Lepidus to retire into quiet obscurity.

After defeating Sextus, Octavian enjoyed using the new title conferred on him, Imperator Caesar Divi Filius. Our word *emperor* derives from the Latin *imperator,* but at that time the word only meant commander in chief of the armed forces. The *Divi Filius* part of the title indicated that Julius Caesar had been deified (was considered to be a god), and that Octavian was his son.

With Lepidus out of the way, there were now two rulers of Rome: Octavian and Antony. Before the war with Sextus, Octavian had ordered his sister, Octavia, to marry Antony, hoping this would divert Antony from his deepening love for Cleopatra and his alliance with Egypt. But Octavian's strategy did not work. Antony continued his relationship with Cleopatra and eventually divorced Octavia to marry the Egyptian queen.

Octavian decided it was time for him to fulfill his ambition of becoming the sole ruler of Rome. However, to establish himself in the eyes of the Roman people as worthy of such a position, he had to prove he was a strong military leader and competent general. He launched a campaign against the province of Illyricum (part of modern Slovenia and Croatia) to secure the important trading routes between there and Rome. This time he did not turn to Agrippa to be his main general. Octavian himself led the troops. And not only was he victorious, but he was wounded, an honor that attested to his bravery.

Having established himself as a conqueror and military leader, he obtained a copy of Antony's will and read parts of it at a public forum. What he read disclosed that Antony had bequeathed much of his estate to Cleopatra and her children, two of whom had been fathered by Antony and one by Caesar, whose mistress she had been at the time of the consul's death. This news infuriated Rome's citizens. Knowing how much Romans despised the idea of royalty, Octavian went on to describe how Antony bowed down to Cleopatra; and knowing how Romans prized their own culture above any other, he said that Antony had adopted Egyptian customs and behaved as if he were a king or a god. As Octavian had hoped, the Roman people were so incensed that they were eager to bring down Antony. However, in another clever move, Octavian declared war against Cleopatra, not against Antony, to avoid being accused of starting a civil war against another Roman.

Augustus's forces engage those of Antony and Cleopatra at the Battle of Actium off the coast of Greece in 31 B.C. Augustus soundly defeated the pair, who fled and later committed suicide.

With Agrippa as his second in command, Octavian met Cleopatra's and Antony's forces at sea near Actium in Greece on September 2, 31 B.C. When it became apparent that they faced defeat, first Cleopatra's ship, and then Antony's fled back to Egypt, where they killed themselves—first Antony, and then Cleopatra.

Octavian annexed Egypt as a Roman province. His empire now extended from the Atlantic Ocean in the west, to Asia Minor and the Sahara Desert in the east, and from the Euphrates to the Danube and Rhine Rivers to the north.

Ruler of All Rome

Octavian had Cleopatra's son by Caesar killed, as well as Antony's eldest son. However, he showed compassion by sparing Antony and Cleopatra's twins, whom he brought back to Rome to be raised by his sister Octavia.

Upon returning to Rome, Octavian declared a holiday to celebrate his victories at Illyricum and Actium and his annexation of Egypt. On this occasion he conducted a special ceremony in which he closed the doors of the temple of Janus. Roman tradition held that these doors could be closed only when Rome was at peace, and only twice before in the city's long history had these doors been shut.

Augustus: The Highest

Octavian was a beloved leader and over the next several years he was given many honors and titles. Although he was the undisputed ruler of the Roman world, in 27 B.C., he offered to renounce all his titles and restore the full power of consuls and senators. As he had hoped, the Senate refused his offer. Instead, they bestowed upon him the title of Augustus, meaning the "highest," the "most noble." He could have easily declared himself king or dictator, but remembering the fate of his uncle, he chose instead to be known simply as "princeps" or "first citizen." He was also named governor of Spain, Gaul, and Syria, which were known as the imperial provinces. Over time *princeps* came to mean *prince*. In later years, both *Caesar* and *Augustus* became part of the title assumed by emperors.

Augustus's powers were increased several times by the Senate, as Breasted points out, "not on his demand, for he always showed the Senate the most ceremonious respect, but because the Senate could not dispense with his assistance."[46] Another honor shown Augustus was renaming the month of Sextilius to August. A similar honor had been bestowed on Julius Caesar when the month of Quintilis was renamed July.

In accepting his new titles, Augustus said, "May I be privileged to build firm and lasting foundations for the Government of the State. May I also achieve the reward to which I aspire: that of being known as the author of the best possible Constitution, and

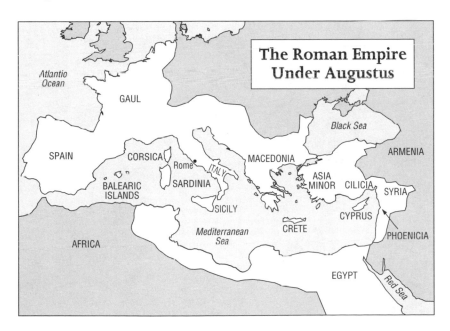

The Roman Empire Under Augustus

of carrying with me, when I die, the hope that these foundations which I have established for the State will abide secure."[47] Augustus would meet his goals.

As ruler of Rome, he embarked on programs to reform the government, the military, and the everyday life of his people. His biggest challenge was maintaining sole power, yet at the same time preserving the forms and traditions of a republic such as elected consuls, senators, and a peoples' assembly. In assessing Augustus as a leader, Tacitus, a historian who wrote about a century after Augustus's death, said, "Indeed, he attracted everybody's goodwill by the enjoyable gift of peace. Then he gradually pushed ahead and absorbed the functions of the Senate, the officials, and even the law."[48]

Sweeping Changes: The Augustan Reforms

Augustus reduced the number of senators, reestablished the peoples' assemblies, and allowed freedom of speech at all meetings. When the Senate was in session, he sat quietly listening to the debates. When he spoke, other senators often disagreed with him, interrupting his speeches with cries of "I don't understand you," and "I'd dispute that point if I got the chance." Though Augustus allowed this freedom of expression, final judgments were always made by him. He did, though, look to trusted advisers for help in

Though Augustus kept traditions of the old Republic, such as the Senate (pictured), and treated the senators with respect, he alone held the ultimate power.

making important decisions. These were his longtime friend Agrippa, his most important general, Maecenas, a wealthy businessman who acted as Augustus's agent for delicate diplomatic errands, and Livia, his wife.

Among his most significant reforms were changes in the army. Before Augustus, armies were raised for specific campaigns and disbanded afterward. Augustus instituted a permanent standing army whose officers served for a given number of years and received regular pay. He enticed recruits by guaranteeing them land and pensions at the end of their enlistment. In later years, those pensioners formed the start of an entire new class of rural farmers in Italy.

Augustus encouraged professionalism and caution in his generals and believed that no campaign or battle should be fought unless the chance of victory was greater than the chance of defeat. Suetonius reported that he compared "those who took great risks in the hope of gaining some small advantage to a man who fishes with a golden hook, though aware that nothing he can catch will be valuable enough to justify its loss."[49] According to Suetonius, the two faults Augustus most hated in a military commander were haste and recklessness. "Give me a safe commander, not a rash one,"[50] he reportedly said.

Augustus also made many reforms in the governing of Rome's provinces. Where before, governors wielded absolute power over their provinces, which Augustus felt invited corruption, he made all governors responsible to him. He ordered censuses to keep track of landownership. And he regulated and collected taxes, which he used for public works and to improve roads. Under his rule, both Rome and the provinces enjoyed prosperity through the security of peace and expanded trade.

Over its long history the city of Rome had grown haphazardly. Streets were narrow and clogged with carts and chariots. The Tiber River was clogged with debris. Most of the buildings were built of plain unadorned brick. Augustus embarked on an ambitious program of improving and beautifying the city.

He imported Greek marble and encouraged the study of Greek architecture. He personally funded the repair of many old buildings and the construction of many new ones. Augustus claimed to have restored eighty-two temples in one year.

Rome was cleaned up. The Tiber was cleared of rubbish and its banks reinforced so ox-drawn barges could haul tons of marble or thousands of bushels of grain to the city docks. Roads were rebuilt. Aqueducts, which delivered water to more than seven hundred public fountains, were repaired and extended. Wealthy citizens

Augustus imported Greek marble and used elements of Greek architecture in his renovation and construction projects in Rome.

were encouraged to underwrite municipal improvements. Under Augustus's urging, Agrippa paid for the reconstruction of the city's sewer system and underwrote the building of Rome's first free public bath. Augustus also established regular police, fire, and water departments within the city. Near the end of his life he said, "I found Rome built of brick; I leave her clothed in marble."[51]

Private Life

Augustus's house was located on the Palatine Hill, an area of Rome that had been home to Rome's early kings and later rulers. In Augustus's time, many wealthy people had elaborate and stately homes there, and though our word "palace" comes from Palatine, Augustus's residence was an older house built of stone and wood, which he remodeled to accommodate his extended family, consisting of himself and his wife, her two sons Tiberius and Drusus, Augustus's daughter Julia, and his sister Octavia and her five children, including Cleopatra's twins. To escape the commotion of such a large household, the emperor spent much of his time in his study on the top level of the house. After his death, his house became a monument and his sleeping room was admired by many generations of Romans.

Augustus entertained often, serving his guests imported delicacies and wines, but his own tastes in food were simple. He liked coarse bread, cottage cheese, lettuce, green figs, and grapes. Often, instead of sitting down to regular meals, he nibbled snacks throughout the day.

As part of his effort to restore traditional values and hoping to set an example for other Romans, he wore simple clothing, which he insisted be spun, woven, and sewn by his wife, sister, or daughter. The women did as he asked, but had their clothes made by dressmakers. To make himself appear taller than his natural five feet, seven inches, Augustus wore lifts in his sandals.

He never completely overcame his physical weaknesses, was prone to catching cold, and was a bit of a hypochondriac. His skin was especially sensitive to the sun, and he never ventured outside without a hat. He hated cold weather and often wore four tunics, one atop another, plus a heavy gown and an undershirt in winter.

Spreads Roman Culture

Alexander had felt Greek culture to be superior to others of his day, and Augustus had the same pride in Roman culture. He wanted Italy to set the example for the rest of the empire. Thus he tried to induce the Roman people to return to what he considered to be the traditional values of religion, family life, and morality, which had suffered much erosion during the past several hundred years. He instituted a number of laws to discourage divorce and

Augustus ruthlessly consolidated his power, but once emperor, he proved himself a wise and capable leader.

adultery, and to encourage marriage and large families. He also reestablished many long-abandoned religious rites and holidays.

Some of these laws later affected his own family. After having been married and divorced or widowed several times in unions made to please her father, his daughter Julia rebelled by having numerous affairs and, once, even held an orgy in a temple. Augustus expelled her to an island for the rest of her life, and later expelled her daughter, also for immoral behavior. But there was more than a bit of hypocrisy in this, for it was well known that throughout his life, Augustus enjoyed extramarital affairs, especially with young women.

Patron of the Arts

In addition to his building programs and civil improvements, Augustus promoted literature and learning. As Alexandria had been the center of learning and culture in Hellenistic times, Rome took over that function in the Augustan Age.

He built a library next to his house and filled it with books from all over the world. Many great Latin poets and writers, such as Virgil, Horace, and Ovid, flourished under his reign. Augustus himself wrote a thirteen-volume autobiography, poems, and at least one play, which he never finished. He commissioned the poet Virgil to compose the *Aeneid*, the classical epic poem telling the legend of Rome's "toga'd people." Many passages of this great work show Augustus as Rome's ultimate hero and savior:

> This, yea, this is the man, so often foretold you in
>   promise,
> Caesar Augustus, descended from God,
> who again shall a golden
> Age in Latium found.[52]

Planning for Heirs

One of Augustus's biggest concerns was the lack of a direct male heir to succeed him. When his daughter had not borne him a grandson by any of her other marriages, he had her marry Agrippa. This union produced not one son, but two, both of whom Augustus legally adopted, hoping to groom at least one to take his place. Unfortunately both boys died before reaching adulthood. There was one other grandson, but because Augustus believed that he would make an unsuitable leader, Augustus exiled him from Rome. Julia was then made to marry Tiberius, one of Livia's sons by her first marriage; but the union produced no children. In desperation, Augustus adopted Tiberius, his stepson, who by then was in his midforties, had always been loyal to Augustus, and had long hoped for this recognition.

Despite Augustus's claim that he had no interest in expanding the borders of the Roman Empire, more territory was added during his reign than at any time before or since. At the end of his reign, the Roman Empire included England, France, Spain, Italy, the lands to the north and east of Italy, the lands surrounding the Mediterranean Sea, the Middle East, Egypt, and Armenia.

In all this time, the imperial armed forces suffered only one military defeat. In 9 B.C., general Quintilius Varus and his three legions were surrounded in a surprise ambush and killed in the Teutoburg Forest in Germany. Augustus was so upset that he did not cut his hair or beard for several months. According to Suetonius, "he hit his head against the door crying, 'Quintilius Varus, give me back my legions.'"[53]

Tiberius was sent to Germany and recovered the territory lost by Varus, but Augustus gave strict orders that no more attempts be made to expand the borders of Roman territory. Even today, the boundary between people who speak Germanic languages and those who speak Latin-based languages remains as it did when Augustus was alive.

Upon his death, Augustus left the empire to Tiberius (pictured).

Augustus received one final honor and title before his death. In the year A.D. 12, he was named pontifex maximus. This title, which means "greatest bridge builder," signified that he not only was the head of state, but also the leader of the Roman religion.

When Tiberius returned from Germany, Augustus named him co-regent. The following year Augustus became ill. He died on August 19 of the year 14, one month before his seventy-sixth birthday. Shortly before his death, he called his family and close friends to him and asked, "Have I played my part in the farce of life creditably enough? If I have pleased you, kindly signify Appreciation with a warm good-bye."[54]

Divine honors were granted Augustus within a month of his death, a precedent that had been set with the earlier deification of Caesar, and one that was to become standard for the emperors who followed. In accordance with one of the emperor's final orders, the *Res Gestae Divi Augusti,* his statements of his own achievements, were inscribed outside his mausoleum.

His full title at his death was Imperator Caesar Divi Filius Augustus, Pontifex Maximus, Consul XIII, Imperator XXI, Tribuniciae Potestatis XXXVII, Pater Patriae. Michael Witoski says of Augustus, "the fact that Tiberius succeeded him without a renewal of internal strife and disastrous civil war is perhaps the best indication of Augustus's success in creating a new and lasting political order."[55]

CHAPTER 4

Attila: King of the Huns

"Speeding hither and thither on their nimble-footed horses, they were filling all the world with panic and bloodshed. When they came, they spared neither religion nor rank nor age, even for wailing children they had no pity."[56] This is how a fifth-century writer described Attila and his Huns. And this is the general picture of the Huns that has been passed down through the ages, so that even today the names *Attila* and *Huns* evoke images of uncivilized barbarian hoards ravaging peaceful villages.

Attila was in fact a "barbarian," a general term used by citizens of the Roman Empire to describe non-Romans. And Attila was uncivilized if judged by Roman and Greek standards. But he was no more savage than any other military leader of his time; thus whether he was civilized depends entirely on how the term is defined.

The Huns did not live in fine houses with indoor plumbing, nor did they have centuries of tradition recorded in literature as did the Romans. But the Huns had a distinctive culture. And according to Romans who knew Attila, although he could neither read nor write, he spoke not only his own language and those of other barbarian tribes, but Latin and Greek as well. He was intelligent, well liked, and respected by those who knew him. Historian Edward Gibbon, author of the eighteenth-century classic, *The Decline and Fall of the Roman Empire,* quotes a description written about a hundred years after the death of Attila:

> His features, according to the observation of a Gothic historian, bore the stamp of his national origin . . . a large head, a swarthy complexion, small, deep-seated eyes, a flat nose, a few hairs in the place of a beard, broad shoulders, and a short square body, of a nervous strength, though of a disproportion form. The haughty step and demeanour of the king of the Huns expressed the consciousness of his superiority above the rest of mankind; and he had a custom of fiercely rolling his eyes, as if he wished to enjoy the terror which he inspired. . . . He delighted in war; but, after

he had ascended the throne in a mature age, his head, rather than his hand, achieved the conquest of the North; and the fame of an adventurous soldier was usefully exchanged for that of a prudent and successful general.[57]

Priscus, a Greek historian who visited Attila at his court and wrote an extensive history of him, said he "was a man born to shake the races of the world."[58]

Earliest Huns

The Huns arrived in central and eastern Europe sometime in the middle of the fourth century. No one is sure exactly where they came from, but most historians feel they may have originated as the Hsiung-Nu, a tribe that fought the rulers of ancient China, demanding tributes of gold, silk, and female slaves. Edward Gibbon wrote, "A select band of the fairest maidens of China was annually devoted to the rude embraces of the Huns."[59]

The Hsiung-Nu were driven out of China at the beginning of the first century B.C. and began a long westward migration. Whether they were the ancestors of the Huns is not certain, but it is known that the Huns maintained trading ties with China and that their small shaggy-maned horses were a Mongolian breed rather than the sleeker breeds found in Europe.

The early Huns were nomads who traveled with their herds of horses, cattle, and sheep, camping in various temporary sites in circular domed tents called yurts, which were made of skins and felt stretched over collapsible wooden frames.

Attila, king of the Huns.

The Huns were fierce fighters who raided other tribes, stealing women, weapons, gold, and whatever else they could take. Their skill in horsemanship was such that they were said to do everything from the saddle, including conducting negotiations, sleeping, and even performing necessary bodily functions. One observer said, "not even the centaurs grew closer to their horses."[60]

The Huns may have invented the stirrup, which was unknown at that time in Europe. This gave a distinct advantage in fighting, for with feet braced in stirrups and lower legs gripping the horse's body, a rider was secure enough to stand up and use both hands to shoot the highly specialized Hun reflex bow.

Patrick Howarth, a leading authority on the Huns, says "Not the least of the reasons why the Huns inspired so much terror was the speed of their movements."[61] The first warning of an attack on a village was a cloud of dust and the pounding of horses' hooves, followed immediately by a rain of arrows darkening the sky.

At the end of the fourth century, the Roman historian Ammianus Marcellinus said:

> When attacked . . . they fill the air with varied and discordant cries. They fight in no regular order of battle, but by being extremely swift and sudden in their movements, they disperse, and then rapidly come together again in loose array, spread havoc over vast plains, and flying over the rampart, they pillage the camp of their enemy almost before he has become aware of their approach.

> It must be owned that they are the most terrible of warriors because they fight at a distance with missile weapons [arrows] having sharpened bones admirably fastened to the shaft. When in close combat with swords, they fight without regard to their own safety, and while their enemy is intent upon parrying the thrust of the swords, they throw a net over him and so entangle his limbs that he loses all power of walking or riding.[62]

Romans of Attila's time portrayed him as a brutal savage, and later historians perpetuated this infamous reputation.

The land over which the Huns traveled was inhabited by a number of different Germanic tribes such as the Alans, Ostrogoths, and Visigoths. To the south, west, and southeast lay the Roman Empire, whose borders had remained largely unchanged since the days of Augustus in the early first century, except that in 395 the empire had split into western and eastern divisions.

In their continuing westward migrations, the Huns formed temporary alliances with one tribe or another, sometimes to attack other tribes and sometimes to raid Roman border towns. Most tribes fought exclusively on horseback, a practice that changed the way wars would be fought for the next thousand years. While the Huns did not invent the use of mounted troops—the Persians had an efficient cavalry even in the time of Alexander—foot soldiers constituted the bulk of the Roman fighting forces until it became necessary to use more cavalry in response to the barbarian attacks. H. L. Oerter, a history professor, has noted, "Not until the development of gunpowder and the introduction of firearms onto the battlefield was this notion [of the primacy of infantry] questioned—and even then it took the better part of two centuries to effect a change."[63]

Since the Huns left no accounts of their history, the only records we have of them are those written by citizens of the Roman Empire, who viewed the eastern invaders as something

The Huns' swift mounted attacks wreaked havoc on the Romans and other enemies.

less than human. Marcellinus also wrote, "The Huns exceed anything that can be imagined in ferocity and barbarism. They gash their children's cheeks to prevent their beards growing. Their stocky body, huge arms, and disproportionately large head give them a monstrous appearance. They live like beasts."[64]

Attila's Early Years

Attila was born around A.D. 400. His grandfather was Balamber, an earlier ruler of the Huns, who had four sons, Mundzuk, Oktar, Ruga, and Aybars. Nothing is known of Oktar and Aybars, but Mundzuk and Ruga were Balamber's successors. Mundzuk was the elder, and he had two sons, Attila and Bleda. A Hun legend tells that Balamber named his grandson for the Volga River, known in the Hun language as the Atil, which was considered the father of all rivers.

Mundzuk was sickly and died when Attila and Bleda were young. Then Mundzuk's brother Ruga became ruler, and it was he who raised Attila and Bleda. Like most Hun children, Attila learned to ride a horse before he could walk, and by the time he was five he could wield a saber. He learned the history of his people by listening to stories and ballads, but had no formal schooling.

By this time the Huns no longer lived in yurts, but built simple wooden houses in villages in Pannonia (Hungary). As leader of the Huns, Ruga often received diplomatic delegations from the Eastern Roman Empire as well as from other tribes. Attila sat in on these meetings and learned much from them about life in the Roman Empire and about the ancient Greeks and Persians and their empires.

An earlier ruler of the Huns had established the custom of exchanging young boys as hostages with the Roman Empire as one means of assuring peace. Ruga continued this practice, and when Attila was around ten years old, Aetius, a young Roman, was sent to live with the Huns. Attila would be sent to Ravenna, then the capital of the Western Roman Empire, but not until he was twelve.

As a hostage, Aetius could not leave the Huns' camp, but he was not treated like a prisoner. He was treated much the same as Attila and learned the Hun language, customs, and methods of warfare. He also became good friends with Attila. Later, Aetius would become a leading Roman general, sometimes the ally of Attila and sometimes his foe.

When Attila was in Ravenna, he learned to speak Latin and Greek and became familiar with the Roman way of life. He rejected that life early on, however, deciding that the amenities enjoyed by Romans, such as finely woven clothing, elaborate stone houses with elegant furnishings, and delicate foods, were not necessary for a Hun. According to a nineteenth-century French historian, he was taken with "the incompetence of their [Roman] emperors, the corruption of their statesmen, and the absence of morality among their masses."[65]

In due time Attila returned to the Huns and Aetius to the Romans, and while Attila was leading raids against other tribes and strengthening his position as a future leader of his people, Aetius was working his way up in the Roman army. About the friendship between Attila and Aetius, a French historian said, "These two men respected each other, and secretly even feared each other. They were like two rivals, who knew that perhaps one day they would have to face one another on the battlefield. They also believed only they were worthy to measure each other's strength."[66]

The Decline of Rome; The Rise of the Huns

The Roman Empire was not as strong as it had been in earlier days. Not only were its borders being broached by barbarians, but within the empire there was continual political turmoil. And while people valued their status as Roman citizens, many Romans did not want to serve in the army. Because of this, and because so many barbarians had settled in the empire, Roman armies were staffed more by barbarian mercenaries and less by Romans.

Ruga and his Huns had become a real threat to the Eastern Empire and made many attacks against its borders. Hoping to keep Ruga from his gates, Emperor Theodosius II agreed to pay Ruga a tribute of 350 pounds of gold a year. Meanwhile, Ruga continued to lead his Huns on raids on other tribes, and the Romans continued to have trouble with other barbarians who were invading the northern extremities of the empire. In 433 Aetius, now a Roman general, asked Ruga to send him troops to strengthen his army in Italy. In return, Aetius arranged for the land on which the Huns were living to be formally ceded to them as their permanent homeland.

Ruga died in 434 and was succeeded by Bleda and Attila, who ruled together for around ten years. Bleda ruled the western part of Hun territory while Attila concentrated on the eastern portions. However, when Theodosius decided that Ruga's death meant he no longer had to pay the tribute to the Huns, the brothers called for a meeting with the emperor. The meeting took place where the Morava and Danube Rivers meet, in today's Slovakia, and was held entirely on horseback in the Hunnic custom. This undoubtedly was an uncomfortable position for the Romans, who were used to conducting affairs of state around a table or at a forum. Whether because of the discomfort of negotiation from the saddle or the threats of the Hunnic brothers, Theodosius agreed not only to continue paying the tribute, but to increase it from 350 to 700 pounds. The Romans also agreed to return all Hun hostages, to refrain from entering into alliances with tribes

Theodosius II, ruler of the Byzantine, or Eastern Roman, Empire.

fighting against the Huns, and to cancel any agreements that already existed. Furthermore, the Romans agreed to establish free trade for Hun merchants along the Danube, guaranteeing them the same rights and privileges granted to Roman merchants. This agreement, known as the Treaty of Margus, was a huge victory for the Huns.

After this treaty, Attila remained in the east, where he conquered new territories, extending the Hunnic empire into central Asia and Persia. Upon his return to Pannonia, he joined his brother in a new attack against the Eastern Empire that began when Bleda claimed that the bishop of Margus had entered Hun territory illegally and had stolen treasures from Hunnic graves. Important Huns were often buried with some of their gold, weapons, and other valuable personal belongings. Attila and Bleda also accused the Romans of continuing to hold Hun hostages. The brothers went on to wrest from the Eastern Empire most of what today comprises Yugoslavia, Bulgaria, and Greece. Hun forces even reached Constantinople, the capital of the Eastern Empire, but were unable to breach its strong fortresslike walls.

By 438, when Attila was commanding eastern Hun forces, the Romans were busy trying to secure their three-thousand-mile-long border. The Vandals, another barbarian tribe, had conquered northern Africa, giving them control over Carthage, one of the major trade cities on the Mediterranean Sea, and they were now threatening Sicily. In addition to fighting the barbarians in the south and west, the Romans were also fighting the Persians in the east. Attila took advantage of this dissipation of Roman forces to carry out raids against the border of the Eastern Roman Empire.

Theodosius again pleaded for peace and was again forced to capitulate to the Huns' terms, set forth in what was called the First Peace of Anatolius. He agreed to pay a penalty of six thousand pounds of gold, and his annual tribute was raised to a thousand pounds. Soon after concluding this treaty, Bleda died. Some accounts say that he died in a hunting accident, while others attribute his death to Attila. At any rate, Attila became the sole ruler of the Huns in 443.

Attila as Ruler

Attila controlled much of central Europe and was the most powerful ruler in Europe outside the Roman Empire. No longer were his people nomads. They had settled into their homeland and had become, for the most part, farmers. Attila employed as advisers many Romans, who helped him better understand the ways and

Attila, a brilliant military strategist as well as a cunning warrior, quickly conquered large chunks of the Eastern Roman Empire.

means of his enemies. Also, he changed his methods of warfare, adding divisions of infantry to augment his cavalry, with the result that his army became more like that of the Romans. He placed himself on a par with the Roman emperors and spent much of his effort in diplomatic negotiations with them.

But his days of marauding attacks were far from over. In 447 he made a new attack against the Eastern Empire, devastating much of the area between the Black and Mediterranean Seas. Of this campaign, an early Christian historian wrote, "The barbarian nation of Huns, which was in Thrace [part of present day Greece], became so great that more than a hundred cities were captured. There were so many murders and blood-lettings that the dead could not be numbered. Ay, for they took captive the churches and monasteries and slew the monks and maidens in great quantities."[67]

Although Attila was nowhere near the Eastern capital of Constantinople, the people of that city feared his coming. Their fears were strengthened when an earthquake, followed by several days of unrelenting rain, destroyed much of the city, its protective walls, and the towers surrounding it. Theodosius ordered the walls rebuilt, but nonetheless, many people fled.

Theodosius's new commanding officer, a German named Arengliscus, took the offensive and marched to meet Attila. The opposing forces clashed in Thrace, and Arengliscus was killed. Though Attila's forces suffered heavy losses, he won the day. He went on to lay waste to much of Greece, but never did make a direct attack on Constantinople. Historians have long speculated on this uncharacteristic failure to press an advantage. One thought is that the Hun ruler was aware of the city's recently rebuilt walls and knew that his forces did not have the necessary equipment to demolish them. But the more likely reason is one that plagued all armies from ancient to quite recent times—diseases such as malaria and dysentery had killed more men than the actual fighting, and had weakened those who survived. So Attila returned to his home base and began three years of new negotiations with Theodosius. Emissaries traveled back and forth between the Hun camp and Constantinople, and in the process Attila received many lavish gifts. In the end, once again Theodosius was humbled before the Hun, finally agreeing to yet another increase in his annual gold tribute and further concessions in land.

Priscus, who was present at these negotiations, was much impressed with the elaborate court rituals. He was equally impressed with the high degree of refinement evident in the Huns' living arrangements and furnishings, and with Attila's personal rejection of many of these refinements:

A bard entertains Attila and fellow Huns at a banquet.

All the chairs were ranged along the walls of the house on either side. In the middle sat Attila on a couch, another couch being set behind him. At the back of this steps led up to his bed, which was covered with white linens and colored embroideries for ornament.

While sumptuous food, served on silver plates had been prepared for the other barbarians and for us, for Attila there was nothing but meat on a wooden platter. He showed himself temperate in all other ways too, for gold and silver goblets were offered to the men at the feast, but his mug was of wood.

His dress was plain, having care for nothing other than to be clean, nor was the sword by his side, or the clasps of his barbarian boots, nor the bridle of his horse, like those of the Scythians, adorned with gold or gems or anything of high price.[68]

Priscus also wrote about Attila's principal wife, Kreka, noting that her quarters included "numerous buildings, some of carved boards beautifully fitted together, others fastened on round wooden blocks, which rose to a moderate height from the ground."[69]

Though Priscus held the usual Roman prejudices against barbarians, the more he came to know Attila, the more he respected him. He was impressed with Attila's personal habits of temperance and moderation, his intelligence, and the conduct of Attila and his entire court.

Within his own country, Attila was not only the king and commander of the army, he was also judge and jury for both civil and criminal offenses committed by his own people. Complaints were brought before him from the farthest reaches of his empire. The parties would come before him and state their case, and he would hand down a judgment.

It is apparent from the writings of Priscus and other contemporaries that Attila presided over a complex court system, different from that of the Romans, but as replete with elaborate conventions as that of any ruler of an empire. Much of the court etiquette surrounding Attila was reminiscent of the customs of the desert kings of Persian cultures.

Plot Against Attila

The next few years were eventful ones in Attila's life. In 449, he uncovered a plot against his life. The assassination plot was a devious one. Theodosius, tired of paying tributes to Attila, arranged for Roman officials to bribe one of Attila's emissaries to Constantinople to murder Attila. But the plan backfired when Attila's man proved loyal and reported the offer to his chief. Attila ordered the Romans back to Constantinople, but without revealing his knowledge about the plot. He also sent his own emissaries, who made the plot known in front of Theodosius's entire court. Once again, Attila had triumphed over Theodosius, who then had to pay even higher costs in tributes and gifts.

Not long after that final humiliation, however, Theodosius died. Marcian, the emperor who replaced him, refused either to pay the tributes or to enter into negotiations with Attila. Attila did not pursue the matter because around that time events occurred that ended up providing him with a unique opportunity to make war against the Western Empire.

Those events involved a love affair between Honoria, the sister of Valentinian, the Western emperor, and a minor court official.

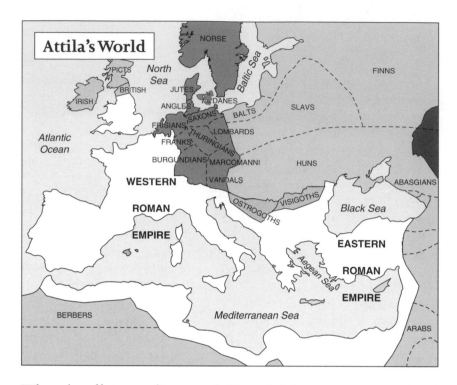

When the affair was discovered, Honoria's lover was executed and arrangements were made for Honoria to marry an old man. Honoria refused the marriage and was shunted off to Constantinople, where she could be watched more closely. But Honoria wanted her freedom, and she concocted a wild plan: she sent a messenger to Attila agreeing to marry him if he would rescue her from her plight.

A match between the most ferocious of the barbarians and the sister of a Roman emperor was an unlikely one, and no one knows how serious Honoria was, or for that matter, whether Attila really wanted her for a bride. But Attila immediately recognized the bargaining power he now held and he decided to use it. He sent a message to Valentinian demanding Honoria and half the Western Empire as her dowry. No doubt he knew his demand would be refused. And when it was, he marched against Valentinian.

The Roman commander in chief for this war was none other than Attila's boyhood friend Aetius, who was now Valentinian's chief political adviser and the Western Empire's leading general.

Both Attila and Aetius augmented their respective forces. Valentinian allied with the Visigoths, the Burgundians, and one faction of Franks, while Attila allied with an opposing faction of Franks, the Ostrogoths, the Vandals, and the Alans.

As Attila led his troops over the Roman border into Gaul, people trembled in fright. Many legends have grown up in Christian folklore about those few souls brave enough to face the Scourge of God, as Attila had become known. One of the most famous is the story of St. Genevieve, a young girl from the then small city of Paris, who offered to face this supposedly archenemy of Christendom by herself. She prayed and urged the people not to flee, prophesying that Paris would be spared. She was correct. Attila bypassed Paris and instead led his army to the Catalunian Fields, a large open area well west of the city, near Chalons.

There, the armies of Aetius and Theodoric, king of the Goths, faced Attila's army in one of the largest and most savage battles in history. The two armies were well matched, both in numbers and in leadership. Contemporary accounts give figures that range between 300,000 and 700,000 for the army of the Huns, and similar numbers for the Romans and Goths. A sixth-century historian described the battle as "a conflict fierce, various, obstinate and bloody, such as could not be paralleled in either the present or in past ages."[70]

In readying his troops for battle, Attila reportedly said:

> Now show your cunning, Huns, now your deeds of arms. Let the wounded exact in return the death of his foe. Let the unwounded revel in slaughter of the enemy. No spear shall harm those who are sure to live, and those who are sure to die fate overtakes even in peace. And finally, why

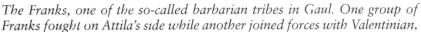

The Franks, one of the so-called barbarian tribes in Gaul. One group of Franks fought on Attila's side while another joined forces with Valentinian.

should fortune have made the Huns victorious over so many nations unless it were to prepare them for the joy of this conflict. . . . I shall hurl the first spear at the foe. If any man can stand at rest while Attila fights, he is a dead man.[71]

Fighting was hand to hand and fierce. The Goth historian Jordanes depicted the scene as "a stream being turned into a torrent of human blood" and observed that "those whose wounds drove them to slake their parching thirst drank water mingled with gore."[72]

After almost a full day of combat, both sides were exhausted. Theodoric was killed, and his men slowly left the battlefield. Eventually the fighting petered out, with both Aetius and Attila withdrawing their forces. Losses were extraordinary. One source estimates that between 200,000 and 300,000 bodies lay strewn over the field. Although there was no clear winner of the battle, this was Attila's first major setback. He had been driven out of Gaul and the Roman Empire, and he seems to have abandoned his quest for Honoria.

Sir Edward Creasy, a professor at the University of London in 1840, designated the Battle of Chalons as one of fifteen of the world's most decisive military encounters. Many agree and believe that this battle helped to determine the religious direction of Europe after the Roman Empire. In the fourth and fifth centuries, the practice of Christianity was growing rapidly, but only within the Roman Empire. The Huns, and most of the other Germanic tribes,

After a bloody battle against his childhood friend Aetius, Attila retreated and gave up his quest to conquer Gaul.

still worshiped ancient gods of nature. So it is probably true that if Attila had won and had gone on to conquer Gaul, the future of Europe would have been determined more by non-Christians than by Christians. Also, the failure of the Huns in general and Attila specifically to embrace Christianity "was certainly one of the reasons why contemporary and near-contemporary chroniclers in general wrote so disparagingly about the Huns."[73]

Invasion of Italy

Attila brought his weary troops home to Hungary and renewed his demands for tribute from Marcian, the new Eastern emperor, who refused to acquiesce. Still smarting from his defeat in Gaul, Attila was not about to accept this refusal meekly. He once again readied his troops for a long march and invaded Italy, ravaging at least twelve cities on the way to Rome. The Huns met little resistance in northern Italy, partly because Eastern Roman troops were engaged in campaigns elsewhere and Aetius's troops from the Western Empire were still recuperating from the losses they had suffered at Chalons.

Before Attila reached the Western capital, however, the Romans sent a delegation to meet him, hoping to prevent their city from suffering the fate of those in northern Italy. The emperor knew that if the negotiations were to have any hope of success, Romans of great prestige would have to participate, so he sent Pope Leo I, the head of the Roman Church, and two of Rome's leading senators.

After the meeting, Attila withdrew his army and returned to Hungary. Christians attributed this withdrawal to the presence of the pope and the power of God. As with so many other momentous events concerning Attila, Christian legends grew up in years to come to explain this encounter.

One legend was later immortalized by the Renaissance painter Raphael in *The Repulse of Attila,* a mural in the Vatican Palace. In this giant wall painting, St. Peter and St. Paul appear as a vision to Attila during the negotiations, and presumably put the fear of God into the pagan warlord.

It is perhaps more likely, however, that Attila's decision was based on pragmatic considerations, not the least of which was a large payment of gold. Also, disease had killed many of his men. With winter approaching it would be difficult to secure supplies and food for his troops, already seriously weakened in strength and in numbers by dysentery and malaria. Attila knew he would be facing a two-fronted battle against Marcian's army from the east and Aetius's from the west.

Death of Attila

But the day of decisive battle was not to come. Soon after his return to Hungary, in the spring of 453, Attila took a new wife, a Germanic girl named Ildico. After much feasting and drinking, the bridal couple retired to their tent. The next morning neither Attila nor his bride appeared. According to the history recorded by Priscus, "On the following day, when a great part of the morning was spent, the royal attendants suspected some ill and, after a great uproar, broke in the doors. There they found the death of Attila accomplished by an effusion of blood, without any wound, and the girl with downcast face weeping beneath her veil."[74] Attila apparently had had a bloody nose, a condition to which he was prone, and had died from suffocation. It is obvious from this account that no one suspected Ildico of foul play, but in later years Ildico was suspected.

Attila was mourned in the usual Hun fashion. His body was laid out on a silk-covered bier. The men sheared off their long hair and lacerated their faces, then mounted their horses and galloped around the body "to gladden the heart of the dead leader."[75]

There are two versions of the burial. According to Jordanes, "They bound his coffins, the first with gold, the second with silver, and the third with the strength of iron. The three coffins were probably a way of honoring Attila. They also added the [swords] of foemen won in the fight, trappings of rare worth, sparkling with gems, and ornaments of all sorts. . . . That so great riches might be kept from human curiosity they slew those appointed to the work, a dreadful reward for their labour."[76]

But according to Hungarian legend and tradition, Attila's servants first dammed the Zaguyal River, near the city of Jászberény in modern-day Hungary, then placed his body in the opening, and immediately undammed the river so that his body would lie forever covered with water. No one has ever claimed to have found his burial place.

After Attila

Attila had ruled the Huns alone for only eight years, but during that time he gained control over much of eastern and central Europe and seriously threatened both the Western and Eastern Roman Empires. Certainly his raids contributed to the further weakening and disintegration of the Western Empire, which collapsed completely in 476.

Attila was succeeded by his eldest son, but the leadership of Ellak was almost immediately challenged by his brothers. In 454,

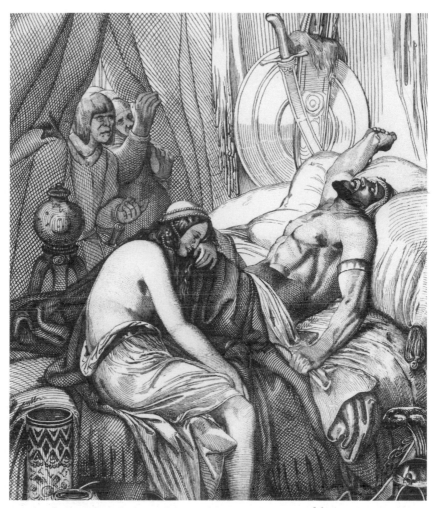

Attila died in his sleep on his wedding night, most likely of suffocation resulting from a bloody nose.

only one year after Attila's death, the Ostrogoths and other Germanic tribes living under the Huns' rule revolted. The Hun empire came to an end in 469, when one of Attila's sons was killed and his head brought to Constantinople, where it was carried in procession through the streets and fixed on a pole for all to see.

Attila's youngest son, Irnak, who became known in Hungarian legends as Prince Casaba, made peace with the Eastern emperor and brought a small remnant of his people to what is today Bulgaria where, according to Hungarian legends, they merged with the ancestors of the Magyars and became the Hungarian nation. And, even today, in Hungary, Attila (known there as Ethele), is a great national hero.

CHAPTER 5

Charlemagne: First Holy Roman Emperor

"Long life and victory to Charles Augustus, crowned by God the great and pacific Emperor of the Romans,"[77] roared the large crowd in St. Peter's Cathedral on Christmas Day in Rome in the year 800.

On that day, Charles, also known as Charles the Great, Carolus Magnus, Karl der Grosse—or Charlemagne, was crowned as the first Roman emperor since the fall of the old Western Roman Empire, 324 years earlier. From then on this monarch would be known as the Holy Roman Emperor, and the office would exist until the time of Napoleon Bonaparte.

Long before becoming emperor, Charles had ruled a vast domain that extended from the Atlantic coast of present-day France to the Danube River in present-day Austria. J. Kelley Sowards of

Pope Leo III crowns Charles Holy Roman Emperor on Christmas Day in 800.

Wichita State University says, "He vanquished and made tributary all the wild and barbarous tribes dwelling in Germany between the Rhine and the Vistula, the Ocean and the Danube."[78]

Historians have called the Europe of Charles's time the Dark Ages, for with the old empire, a unified network of provinces, in which travel, trade, architecture, and learning had flourished, deteriorated into separate warring Germanic kingdoms. Most of the Roman roads and aqueducts fell into disuse and disrepair, as did the magnificent buildings and baths. Though some Roman culture was retained through small numbers of upper-class nobles and churchmen who spoke Latin and studied classical literature, most people were illiterate and knew nothing of the past glories of Rome and Greece. But the darkness that covered Europe did not extend to the Byzantine Empire (once the Eastern Roman Empire) or the Islamic lands in Spain, North Africa, and the Middle East, where learning and culture continued to flourish.

Charles is noteworthy because he strove to restore some of the legacy of Rome and Greece to his subjects. He built new roads and reestablished trade across central Europe. He brought Byzantine and Islamic artists, architects, and sculptors to his court. But he is remembered most for his fostering of knowledge and learning. It was under his direction that many monks undertook the task of copying, restoring, and preserving ancient manuscripts of classical Latin and Greek literature.

Unfortunately, most of Charlemagne's accomplishments were lost in the centuries following his death, remaining hidden for another half millennium, when the Renaissance would revive a high level of culture and learning in Europe.

Birth and Youth

Charles was born on April 2, 742, the son of Pepin the Short and his wife, Bertrada. Pepin, like his father before him, was the mayor of the palace in the court of Franks, a Germanic people who had settled in what is today western Germany and northern France. Once part of the Roman province of Gaul, this region was renamed Frankland in 507 by King Clovis. Clovis's descendants reigned for around two hundred years, but by the early 700s they had become figureheads in their own court, with true power being wielded by the mayor of the palace. Einhard, a member of Charlemagne's court, wrote, "There was nothing left for the King to do but . . . sit on his throne and play the ruler."[79]

In 754 Pepin sent a message to Pope Stephen in Rome, telling him that the current king, Childeric III, was too feeble minded to

Pepin is proclaimed king of the Franks.

rule. The pope needed Pepin's military support to defend Rome against the Lombards, another Germanic tribe that had settled in the north of Italy, so he officially deposed Childeric and anointed Pepin as the new king.

According to Frankish court records, twelve-year-old Charles performed his first royal duty when he greeted the pope and headed the ceremonial march back to the palace. Pepin's coronation began the Franks' close relationship with the papacy which, under Charles, would become even stronger. France's papal ties lasted until the time of Napoleon.

Very little is known about Charles's boyhood, but Einhard says he "gave himself eagerly to riding and hunting, arts into which he was, as a Frank, born."[80] Young Charles was schooled in warfare, learning to handle weapons such as the spatha (a heavy, long-bladed sword), scramasax (a curved knife), and battle-ax. In addition, as a son of the royal household, he probably was tutored in grammar, logic, rhetoric, arithmetic, music, astronomy (astrology), and geometry. The grammar would have been classical Latin, the formal language of educated people. The everyday language spoken by Charles and other Franks was a mixture of early German and a colloquial Latin that evolved into French.

There is some controversy over whether Charles ever learned to write. Referring to Charles as an adult, Einhard says: "He tried to write, and used to keep tablets and blanks in bed under his pillow, that at leisure hours he might accustom his hand to form the letters; however, as he did not begin his efforts in due season, but late in life, they met with ill success."[81]

Some historians feel this remark applied not to everyday writing but to the highly specialized calligraphy reserved for the copying of manuscripts. This script was developed by the monks employed by Charles to copy ancient Roman and biblical texts and is the basis of our lowercase letters (modern capital letters come from ancient Latin). Writing aside, Einhard also said, "Charles had the gift of ready and fluent speech and could express whatever he had to say with the utmost clearness, [and] was such a master of Latin that he could speak it as well as his native tongue; but he could understand Greek better than he could speak it."[82]

Learning to Be King

When Stephen agreed to crown Pepin, Pepin in turn agreed to come to the aid of the pope, or his successor, if called. In 756 when the Lombards threatened Rome, Pope Stephen did call on Pepin, who led his army across the Alps and south to Rome. Charles gained experience in battle when he accompanied his father and the Frankish troops in this successful action against the Lombards.

Pepin died in 768, and the kingdom was divided between twenty-six-year-old Charles and his brother Carloman. The terms of the will stated that each brother was to rule his own domain, but the two were to come to each other's aid as necessary. A few months after Pepin's death, the people of Aquitaine, a large region in the southern part of Charles's lands, revolted. Charles called for his brother's help, but Carloman refused. Charles put down the revolt himself, and relations between the brothers were never mended. Carloman died after a short illness three years later, leaving Charles in sole charge of their father's domain.

Conquests and Building an Empire

Charles was now ruler of the area today comprising France, Belgium, the Netherlands, part of western Germany, and some of Switzerland. He wanted more and had plans to include Bavaria, ruled by his cousin Tassilo, in his domain. But before he could attend to Bavaria, he had to deal with the Saxons, longtime enemies of the Franks, whose lands bordered Frankland to the south and east. Unlike the more southern Germanic tribes, the Saxons had never been Romanized and had never converted to Christianity. There had been a truce between the Saxons and Franks since the last years of Pepin's reign, but in 772 they broke the peace by raiding Frankish villages and burning homes and churches.

Charles called his council of lords and these advisers agreed that war was necessary. Charles's army made brutal attacks on Saxon villages and destroyed the Irminsul tree, an important pagan shrine. Though the Saxons were fierce fighters, their strong suit was guerrilla warfare, and they were no match for Charles's traditionally trained troops. Charles was victorious, but this was only to be another temporary truce.

In 774 current pope Hadrian I sent a message requesting Charles's help in repelling the Lombards, who were once again threatening Rome. Charles marched his troops over the Alps, attacking one Lombard city after another. Most fell easily; but Pavia, where the Lombard king lived, held out. Charles used siege tactics, blockading the city for months until Pavia surrendered.

Meanwhile, Charles left part of his army in Pavia and led the remainder south to conquer the rest of Lombard. It was close to Easter, and Charles decided to celebrate his triumph with a pilgrimage to Rome. The visit would cement his ties with Pope Leo III who had assumed the papacy in 795 after Hadrian's death. The pilgrimage also would demonstrate the Frankish ruler's devotion to the church. In Rome, Charles was greeted as a great hero and feted with parades and banquets. During his visit he proclaimed himself the new king of Lombard. He returned to Pavia, where he banished the conquered Lombard king to a monastery. With the territories he had won in Italy and Pavia, Charles was now the most powerful king in Europe other than the Byzantine emperor.

While Charles had been away from home, the Saxons had renewed their raids into Frankish territory, this time under a strong new leader, Widikind. Charles was tired of the continuing skirmishes with the Saxons; he wanted peace, and he decided that the best way to achieve this was to convert the Saxons to Christianity. According to the Frankish annual records for 775, he resolved "to wage war upon the perfidious and oathbreaking Saxon people until they were conquered and converted to the Christian religion, or totally annihilated."[83]

He was victorious in this fight, but the Saxons continued to plague him for over twenty years before he was able to completely subdue them. During that time he also became embroiled in a war between Muslims who occupied a large part of Spain and their

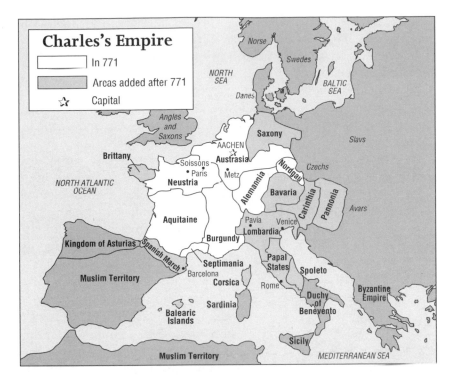

Charles's Empire

In 771

Areas added after 771

☆ Capital

overlords in the Near East. However, the fighting in Spain did not go well for the Franks and, for the first time since he had become king, Charles was forced to retreat.

A Brief Respite

Back home from Spain, Charles had a brief respite from waging war and devoted himself to affairs within his own lands. He was, at this time, married to his third wife, Hildegarde, having divorced the first two. He had one son from his first marriage, a boy who had a hunchback so severe that he was considered unsuitable as an heir to the throne. Hildegarde, however, bore him several children, including Louis, who eventually succeeded Charles. Although Hildegarde was only thirteen when she married Charles, who was thirty at the time, the union was a happy one. Richard Winston, a modern biographer of Charles, notes, "It was she [Hildegarde] who surrounded him with that bustling family atmosphere that he loved, that provided the proper counterpoint to the necessarily grim business of ruling and expanding domain."[84]

In private life he was said to be a man of gentle nature. According to Einhard, "Charles was firm and steady in his human relationships, developing friendships easily, and doing everything he possibly could for anyone whom he had admitted to this degree of intimacy."[85] Einhard also spoke of Charles's relationships with his children: "He paid such attention to the upbringing of his sons and daughters that he never sat down to table without them when he was at home, and never set out on a journey [other than war] without taking them with him."[86] He was so attached to his daughters that he would not allow them to marry unless their husbands agreed to reside within his court, but he was indulgent of them and overlooked the many love affairs the girls had.

As well as spending time with his family, Charles also turned his attention to intellectual and artistic pursuits. He instituted a school at his court for his own children and also for children of noblemen and commoners alike. The head teacher, Alcuin, was a highly acclaimed English scholar who attracted artists and goldsmiths, as well as poets, writers, astronomers, mathematicians, musicians, architects, philosophers, and theologians as teachers in Charles's school. Under Alcuin's direction, Charles accumulated one of the greatest libraries of the time. Alcuin, who was also a bishop, became one of Charles's most trusted advisers.

Charles presides over the palace school. The Frankish king was not only a benefactor of education but also an enthusiastic student himself.

Charles's school was not only for children. Classes were also conducted for the men and women of the court. Charles attended classes in Bible and religious writings as well as in grammar, astronomy, and music.

The adults called their school the Academy, modeling it on the teachings of Socrates and other great classical scholars. During learning sessions, the participants adopted nicknames, often of biblical or classical figures. Einhard wrote that Charles, whose nickname was David, was assured by his fellow students that "his intellectual facilities were broader than the Nile, larger than the Danube and the Euphrates, and no less powerful than the Ganges."[87]

The main objective of education and knowledge in Charles's time was to further religious inquiry and salvation of the soul. As well as providing schools for general learning, Charles also wanted to improve the educational level of local priests, many of whom spoke only minimal Latin and who allowed their congregations to talk during services. He also upgraded the level of religious services, encouraging priests to stop allowing their congregants to talk during the mass. He rebuilt many churches that had fallen into disrepair and were being used for storage barns. He also introduced Gregorian chants as part of the service.

A Return to Conflict

In 782 Charles's respite from war came to an abrupt end when he was compelled to once again face the Saxons, whose leader had returned from Denmark. Still smarting from his defeat in Spain, he was determined, this time, not to be humiliated. He called a meeting with the Saxon chiefs at Verden, a Saxon city on the Aller River and tortured them, forcing them to give him the names of the leaders of the uprising. Charles took immediate action, beheading forty-five hundred Saxons in one day. Winston calls this the "most frightful and dishonorable act of his [Charles's] life."[88] Charles also imposed a number of harsh measures against the Saxons. Most historians believe that later he was truly sorry for his cruelty and that it weighed heavily on his conscience. Many of his own people became disenchanted with him, and the Saxons, hating him even more than before, continued sporadic attacks and underground resistance for another twenty years.

While he was at war with Saxony, Charles lost his wife and his mother in a three-month period. Soon after Hildegarde's death, he married Fastrada, the daughter of an East Frankish noble. The queen of any medieval court was an important personage, but Charles's wife was given an unusual amount of authority and responsibility. Besides supervising the children, she was in charge of overseeing and directing the large court staff and managing domestic affairs.

The battle of Rouncesvilles against the Muslims in Spain was a bitter defeat for Charles.

Around the time of his marriage to Fastrada, Charles discovered two plots to assassinate him. The first was a planned revolt from Thuringia, part of his kingdom near Saxony. Charles lost no time in invading the area, executing the leader, and first blinding, then exiling his cohorts. The second plot came from within his own court and included plans to kill not only him but three of his sons as well. The conspirators wanted to place Charles's crippled son, Pepin, on the throne as a figurehead to be controlled by themselves. Charles executed the leaders and sent Pepin to a monastery for the rest of his life.

With his domestic life regaining normality and threats of conspiracy dispelled, Charles turned once again to empire building. He had always dreamed of uniting all Germanic tribes into one nation. He had made progress in a good part of central Europe, but Bavaria and Pannonia (now Hungary and the Balkan lands formerly comprising Yugoslavia) remained outside his grasp. His long-running dispute with Bavaria was resolved in 788 when he deposed his cousin Tassilo, sent him to a monastery, and annexed Bavaria to Frankland.

Next Charles waged war against the Slavic people, but he allowed them to remain independent after establishing his own areas, called *marches*, along their borders. However, he was not as lenient with the Avars, descendants of or cousins to the Huns, who had ravaged Europe a few hundred years before. "How many battles were fought there and how much blood shed can still be seen by the deserted condition of Pannonia. The place where the palace of the Avar leader stood is so desolate that there is not so much as a trace of human habitation,"[89] reported Einhard. From the Avars, Charles brought back many fabulous treasures of gold, silver, silks, and other items, which would decorate and enrich the great palace he was to build at Aachen. The war against the Avars was to be his last major campaign.

Life in the Palace at Aachen

Before the Avar war, Charles had begun building a great palace at Aachen, a small town in the western part of Germany, which would become the Frankish royal seat. Aachen was chosen because it lay on a site near natural thermal springs and old Roman baths. It was in the center of his realm and situated on an old Roman road still in use, facilitating transportation to other parts of his kingdom. And it was close to the quarries from which building stones were taken. The mineral baths, though, were perhaps the most important attraction to Charles, whose favorite leisure activity was swimming. Records of the time show that when he bathed, he was often joined by his sons and any officials and friends visiting the court. Sometimes over a hundred people would frolic in the baths at the same time.

The palace and accompanying church were magnificent. The throne, carved from a single piece of marble, sat on a raised dais at one end of the palace entrance hall, which was 160 feet long by 60 feet wide. A covered colonnade connected the palace to the church, which was decorated with Roman mosaics, Italian marble, gold, silver, and solid brass doors. Houses for nobles were near the palace, built "just a bit lower than Charles's personal apartments so he could see them from his window."[90]

Charles's carved marble throne sat at the end of a long hall in his palace at Aachen.

Charles rose early and received reports and requests of petitioners while he was getting dressed. After dressing, he attended mass in the royal chapel; then his entire family and retinue rode out to the morning hunt, which was followed by an elaborate noon meal, usually meat from that morning's catch. There was no drinking at these dinners, though, because Charles forbade it. During the meal, guests listened to a poet recite or to a reading from a historical or religious book, often from St. Augustine's *The City of God*, which was the ruler's favorite. After this, there was general conversation and discussion among the guests.

Charles took his responsibilities of ruling his huge realm seriously. He issued decrees specifying exactly how to run his many estates and even ordered that flowers be grown, to decorate churches and to give people the pleasure of looking at them. To oversee his many holdings, he sent *missi dominici* (the lord's emissaries) to check on things and dispense justice. He reportedly said, "I insist, that my missi are, by their upright behavior, examples of the virtues in which they instruct others in my name."[91]

He built new roads and bridges and rebuilt old ones to improve communication and travel. He tried unsuccessfully to build a canal between the Danube and Rhine Rivers, but did succeed in building the first wooden bridge over the Rhine.

A Powerful Arbitrator

Besides administering the daily activities of his realm, Charles was called on to settle disputes, both within his territory and elsewhere. For example, in 795 he was called to Rome because of a dispute between Pope Leo III and a group of clerics who accused him of corruption and immorality. Although Charles did not like Leo, when Leo was attacked and taken prisoner, Charles's fierce faithfulness to his religion and the church prompted him to offer the pope refuge at his court. Donald Bullough, author of *The Age of Charlemagne*, says that by 799, "Charles was head of the world, a man to be acclaimed as the crowning glory of Europe, father of the continent, Augustus; a sovereign with his own capital, a 'second Rome,' worthily provided with buildings; the monarch to whom the chief bishop of the world turned for protection and help."[92] When Leo returned to Rome a few months later, Charles sent two of his own archbishops to conduct an investigation to clear the pope's name.

Charles diligently performed the duties of administering his kingdom, including promoting education, constructing roads and bridges, and settling disputes.

That spring, Charles left Aachen and set out on a long journey, first to tour his entire realm, then to visit Rome. There he planned to check on the investigation into the pope's alleged misconduct and to have his eldest son officially crowned as his successor by the pope.

He arrived in Rome in November 800 and set a date for the pope's trial. After three weeks of deliberations, the jury, made up of churchmen and nobles, was unable to come to a decision. The affair was finally closed when the pope agreed to swear an oath to his innocence. Because Leo was the pope and the head of the Catholic hierarchy, no one contested this. The case was closed and Pope Leo remained in office.

Holy Roman Emperor

Controversy has raged for centuries over whether Charles knew that he was to be crowned the Holy Roman Emperor on December 25, 800. He said he did not, but historians question this because of his elaborate preparations for the visit and the wagons of gold and silver he brought as gifts to the church. Yet Charles himself never took on the title of emperor, wishing to be addressed simply as king of the Franks. He did, however, see himself as defender of the church and of Christianity throughout the world.

To this end, he established friendly relations with the Muslims in Baghdad, hoping to persuade them to stop attacking Christians in neighboring Jerusalem, a holy place in Islam as well as in Christianity and Judaism. His gestures of friendship were well received. The Muslims even sent Charles an elephant as a gift. The elephant, named Abul Abbas, became a favorite of the court and was treated like a family pet, accompanying Charles on his travels until it died eight years later.

One problem that had plagued Charles from the time he was named Holy Roman Emperor was that the Byzantine emperor who controlled much of southern Italy refused to recognize Charles as a fellow emperor. Charles solved the problem by giving up his claim to Venice. In return, the Byzantine emperor finally accepted Charles as his equal.

Weakening of Charles's Empire

Around 810, Charles suffered both personal tragedies and state emergencies. The Vikings were attacking the northern coasts of his realm, a plague was decimating cattle throughout the land, and three relatives died: his sister, his favorite daughter, and one of his sons.

Charles was in despair. He became ill and had trouble sleeping. He also had trouble digesting the roast meats he loved, but he would not follow his doctors' orders to eat them boiled instead.

Years before he had drawn up careful plans for the division of his empire among his sons after his death. Now, thinking of past misdeeds and concerned for his soul, he bequeathed most of his extensive wealth to the church. He also delivered long speeches on vice and piety in public squares. He even considered giving up the kingship and becoming a monk. Then, one more tragedy struck. His eldest son, whom he had hoped would succeed him, died. Many of the royal advisers felt that the remaining son, Louis, would not make a good king and that Charles should pass his kingdom directly to one of his grandsons. But Charles adhered to Frankish tradition and brought Louis from his home in Aquitaine to Aachen, where he spent several months coaching him in his future responsibilities.

The coronation of Charles at St. Peter's Cathedral in Rome.

Thirteen years after his own coronation as Holy Roman Emperor, Charles officially crowned his son Louis as his successor. The ceremony was held at the famous cathedral at Aachen. Charles dressed in his royal robes, which he seldom donned, and gleamed from head to toe with gold and sparkling jewels. After placing the crown on Louis's head, Charles turned to the people and gave a long sermon in which he directed Louis to love and fear God, to protect the church, to be kind to his family, to honor priests, to love the people, to help widows and orphans and the poor, and to be just to all men. Louis agreed. He was

Charles's son Louis was crowned in the palace church at Aachen.

now his father's co-emperor. Charles had not asked the pope to perform the coronation but did it himself, assuming that as Holy Roman Emperor, he had this authority.

The coronation of Louis was Charles's last public act. The following January he contracted a fever, and though he tried fasting to cure himself, he developed pleurisy and died on January 24, 814. He was buried just beneath the entrance to his church, under

Charles's deeds were idealized after his death and he eventually became known as Charlemagne, or Charles the Great.

the west door. The inscription on his tomb reads: "Beneath this stone lies the body of Charles the Great, the Christian Emperor, who greatly expanded the kingdom of the Franks and reigned for forty-seven years."[93]

Physically, Charles must have been an imposing man. Einhard states: "He was tall . . . just about seven times the length of his own feet,"[94] and indeed, when his tomb was opened by archaeologists in 1861, he was measured at close to six and a half feet. Some accounts describe him as looking like the proverbial fairy-tale king with a full head of white hair, a large curling mustache, and long flowing white beard, and most portraits reveal a protruding belly.

After Charles

Charlemagne, as he had come to be called, was mourned throughout Europe, and as time passed a number of stories and legends grew about him. In years to come, he would be idealized in poems and stories and would serve as inspiration and ideal for kings and other great men for centuries to come.

Within forty years of his death, his empire crumbled and most of his accomplishments were lost. Richard Winston describes Charles as "a colossus astride the watershed of history, with one foot in the ancient world, the other in the medieval; a conqueror who ranks with Alexander the Great."[95]

CHAPTER 6

Genghis Khan: Supreme Ruler of All Mongols

In the second half of the twelfth century, central Asia was a vast land encompassing China, great Islamic empires, and an immense inland area of mountains, forests, rivers, steppes (grassy plains), and desert. This was a harsh land, scorching hot in summer, freezing in winter, and always battered by strong winds. There were no great cities or sumptuous palaces. The people lived in clans and tribes and made their living by hunting, fishing, and some farming. The Mongol tribes were nomadic herders of sheep and horses, always traveling over the steppes seeking fresh pastureland.

The Mongols were not one people, but many. Their way of life was as harsh as the land on which they lived. Their entire lives revolved around their small, hardy horses. They used them for transportation across the wide expanses of the steppes. They drank mares' milk and sometimes ate horse meat. They even used horses as currency, trading them for material goods. Paul Ratchnevsky, author of a comprehensive study of Genghis Khan, quotes an ancient Mongol saying: "If the horse dies, I die, if it lives, I survive. What can a Mongol do if he loses his horse?"[96]

Like the Huns of an earlier day, the Mongols lived in collapsible felt tents called yurts, which they set up in camps in different places at different seasons of the year. Each tribe was independent and had its own ruler—or khan. These tribes were in constant conflict, and members often stole one another's wives, slaves, horses, and material goods. Relationships between tribes became a complex web of alliances and enemies, often complicated by blood ties stemming from captured wives and slaves.

But this changed when a young man born on those steppes united all Mongols into one nation and led them to conquer much of the land around them. This man was Genghis Khan, and he amassed one of the largest empires the world has ever known. One historian describes it thus:

Eurasian history begins with the Mongols. Within a few decades of the thirteenth century, they had carved out the most sizable empire in world history, stretching from Korea to Western Russia in the north and from Burma to Iraq in the south. . . . For a generation, the Mongols were masters of much of Eurasia and terrorized the rest.[97]

Birth and Youth

Because Mongols did not keep track of their true birthdays, but celebrated them on any one of the Chinese feast days, most important dates in a ruler's life are approximate. As near as can be determined, the boy who came to be known as Genghis Khan was born around 1165 in the northern area of the present Mongolian People's Republic, near the Onon River.

His father, Yesugei, was not a khan, but was the leader of a small clan that was the remnant of a much larger clan that had been ruled by Yesugei's father. Genghis Khan's mother was Hö'elun, a woman his father had stolen from a rival tribe, the Merkits. The child destined to become the greatest of the Mongols was born on the night Yesugei returned from a victorious raid on another tribe, and, following tradition, he gave his son the name of the defeated chieftain—Temujin. Legend tells that the infant was born clutching a blood clot in the shape of a human knuckle in his tiny fist, and this was interpreted as a sign that he would become a great warrior. The name Temujin also means *iron*, and it is thought the baby had a cradle made of this material.

The traditional dwelling of the nomadic Mongols was the yurt, a tent made of felt.

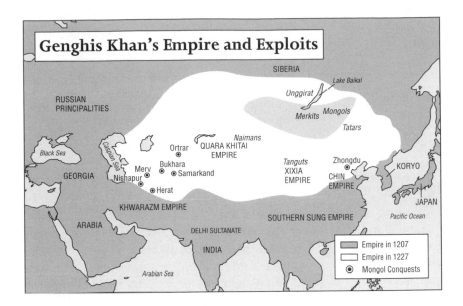

Genghis Khan's Empire and Exploits

Temujin was the first of Hö'elun's children, but she also raised Belgutei and Bektair, Yesugei's sons by an earlier wife. Temujin had several younger brothers and sisters, as well. Like most Mongol children, Temujin learned how to ride, hunt, and fish at a very young age. Ratchnevksy said, "As soon as the children are two or three years old, they begin to ride . . . and then a small bow, suitable in size to their age, is given to them and they are taught to shoot."[98]

Mongol society was a harsh one, and even the games of children reflected this. Once, when he was quite young, Temujin and a close friend, Jamuka, made a pact of fellowship by exchanging gifts and drinking a concoction containing each other's blood. Jamuka gave Temujin a whistling arrow he had carved, and Temujin gave Jamuka an arrowhead he had carved from juniper wood. But childhood did not last long among the Mongols, and by the time Temujin was around nine years old, his father decided it was time to arrange a marriage for the boy.

Father and son set off, intending to travel to the Merkit tribe, hoping to make amends for Yesugei's theft of Hö'elun by asking the Merkits to provide a bride for Temujin. But on the way they visited at a different tribe, where Yesugei saw a girl who, according to the *Secret History of the Mongols,* a book written shortly after Genghis Khan's death, had "a lively face and flashing eyes,"[99] and arranged for betrothal with her instead. The girl's name was Börte. Börte's father accepted on condition that Temujin remain with his people until the couple were of age, a custom often followed among the Mongols.

Yesugei agreed and set off for home. Along the way he came across a camp of Tatars, one of the strongest tribes in the area. All nomadic peoples consider it proper to offer hospitality to travelers, and for travelers to accept this hospitality. So, although the Tatars were traditional enemies of the Mongols, Yesugei stopped and shared their meal. But the Tatars knew who Yesugei was and, treacherously, poisoned his food. Yesugei made it back to his camp but knew he was dying and arranged for a trusted servant to bring Temujin home.

Many of Yesugei's followers did not want Temujin, who was still a child, to become their leader and probably would have killed him, but to do so would have been the first act in a long-lasting blood feud. Instead, knowing that a single family unit separated from the tribe, especially one without a man to protect it, would have a hard time surviving, the tribe abandoned Hö'elun and her children, hoping they would perish. And it was Temujin they were concerned about, rather than his two older stepbrothers, because only the son of a man's number-one wife could inherit his position.

But Hö'elun was strong and determined. For five years she managed to keep her family alive by foraging for small game and having her sons hunt and fish. The *Secret History* records that "Her cap firmly on her head and her dress girt around her knees, she ran up and down the Onon River collecting rowans [berries of the mountain ash] and bird cherries, feeding her chicks day and night."[100]

As his father's principal heir, Temujin saw himself as the leader of his family, and in his own mind, the one to hand out justice when a sibling did something wrong. When Temujin was fourteen, he and his younger brother, Kasar, were fishing and caught a trout. Bektair and Belgutei, the stepbrothers, took the fish from the younger boys and ate it in front of them. Temujin said nothing, but later that day he crept up on Belgutei and killed him with an arrow. Bektair, the younger stepbrother, through either fear or admiration, accepted Temujin's judgment and actions and became a loyal follower of Temujin. Even Temujin's mother accepted this harsh demonstration of Temujin's leadership.

As Temujin grew, other tribes noted his increasing strength and began to plot against him. A rival tribe, the Tayichi'ut, took him as a captive, but feared him so greatly that they kept him in a cage, tied to a wooden harness fastened at the neck and wrists, and assigned special guards to watch over him. Temujin was resourceful, however, and, one night when most of the Tayichi'ut were drinking and feasting in celebration of a holiday, he escaped: "Breaking loose from his gaoler [guard], Temujin struck him on the skull with the cangue [wooden harness] and hid in the bed of the River Onon, lying on his back with only his face projecting from the water."[101] Sorkan-Shira, a man from another tribe who saw the boy in the river, advised him to stay hidden until nightfall, then to run to his mother's tent. Temujin thought of a better plan. He went to Sorkan's tent and asked for help in freeing himself from the harness. Though frightened, Sorkan not only did as he was asked, but hid Temujin in a cart under a load of wool for three days. The help would not be forgotten. Much later, Sorkan was rewarded with land and privileges, and his sons were made generals in the army of Genghis Khan.

Early Adulthood

Now around sixteen years old, Temujin considered himself grown and ready to stake his claim as a leader of men. First, he set out to retrieve Börte, the girl he had been betrothed to seven years earlier, and brought her back to his camp along with her mother. Next, he took his brothers Kasar and Bektair and paid a visit to Toghrul, the chief of the Kerait tribe, who had been an ally of Temujin's father. Temujin knew that by associating himself with Toghrul, he would not only gain the protection of one of the most powerful khans of the steppes, but would enhance his ability to attract a personal following. To show his good faith, he offered as a gift the valuable sable cloak Börte had brought with her as her dowry and said to Toghrul, "In earlier days you swore friendship with my father, Yisugei. Accordingly you are as my own father."[102]

Toghrul was pleased with the gift and accepted the young man as his protégé. "In gratitude for the black sable cloak I will reunite you with your people. I will bring together your dispersed people."[103] The friendship was mutually beneficial. Temujin was backed by Toghrul's power and Toghrul received new faithful followers.

Temujin's strength and leadership emerged early in life.

It was not long before Temujin availed himself of Toghrul's promise. The Merkits decided the time had come to exact retribution for Hö'elun's abduction and attacked Temujin's camp. Temujin and the others fled, but Börte was left behind. Different historians have speculated over why Temujin allowed this. Some say he was so intent on saving his own life that he abandoned his wife. Others say he was shrewd in not exposing himself to danger, knowing he would rescue Börte later. At any rate, Börte was taken by the Merkits, who gave her as wife to the younger brother of the man who had originally been betrothed to Temujin's mother.

Temujin called on Toghrul to help him win back his wife. Toghrul called on Jamuka, Temujin's boyhood friend, who now led his own tribe. Toghrul and Jamuka each agreed to provide a *tuman*, a regiment of around five hundred men, if Temujin could also raise a *tuman*. Temujin, who had only five followers at the time, recruited his first army from among herdsmen from many different tribes. Though most joined at first because of the opportunity to plunder, many stayed with him and became the core of his permanent army.

Once Temujin had amassed his own forces, Toghrul told him they would get Börte back "even if we have to massacre every Merkit."[104] The three-way attack on the Merkits was successful and Börte and Temujin were reunited. Very soon afterward Börte gave birth to a child, who Temujin brought up as his own, even though it was likely that his wife had become pregnant while with the Merkits.

Rise to Power

Temujin had gained riches from Merkit booty, and he had proven himself to be a wise and capable leader who treated his men fairly and generously. It was said of him, "The Prince [Temujin] dresses his people in his own clothes, he permits them to ride his own horses; this man could certainly bring peace to the tribe and rule the nation." Temujin thanked both Toghrul and Jamuka for their support, but also showed his own opinion of himself as being destined for great things. "My strength was fortified by Heaven and Earth. Foreordained [for this] by Mighty Heaven, I was brought here by Mother Earth."[105]

Temujin and Jamuka renewed their friendship, and though each man trained his own troops, they shared one camp. The two men were extremely close, but Jamuka became uneasy about Temujin's growing power. Once, when Jamuka wanted to stop and make camp, Temujin, urged by his wife and mother, continued on. This was a test. Who would the men follow? Many followed Temujin, including many of Jamuka's forces. The fact that so many followed Temujin attested to his personal force and magnetism. He was now a strong leader ready to be considered an equal to other leaders. At a special council of tribes, he was named khan of his newly formed tribe.

Another incident around 1186 permanently severed the tie between Temujin and Jamuka: one of Temujin's men killed Jamuka's younger brother. Though Temujin most likely knew nothing of this random murder, Jamuka gathered his forces and launched a surprise raid on Temujin's camp. Temujin and his men were unprepared for battle and they fled. Jamuka was so angry at not catching Temujin that he ordered the seventy captives he had taken boiled alive in huge cauldrons.

Temujin was then in his twenties, and accounts differ as to his activities during the next several years. Some say he spent them in China, while others say he remained in his own land, but all agree that during those years he was training his forces in a new method of fighting.

He divided his men into units of ten, forming first squads, then squadrons, then thousand-man units called *quarans*, each group having specific functions and duties in battle. Temujin had a great deal of manpower for his time, and often there would be thirteen or more *quarans* fighting together. Scouts, sent ahead of the main force, would draw the enemy into pursuit, leading them directly into the hands of their waiting comrades. With unit leaders communicating their position and movements by means of black and white signal flags, Temujin's army was a formidable force.

About ten years after his defeat at the hands of Jamuka, Temujin was asked by the emperor of the Chin, a Chinese tribe, to come to his assistance against the Tatars, who were raiding their territory. Temujin, in turn, asked Toghrul to join him, and both men were pleased with the opportunity to fight their longtime enemy. Temujin said, "In days gone by the Tartars [Tatars] killed our ancestors and forefathers. We will sacrifice them in revenge and retribution . . . by massacring all except the youngest. They will be massacred down to the very last male and the remainder will be shared out as slaves among us all."[106] Temujin was true to his word. The Tatars were massacred.

As he was leaving the battlefield, Temujin noticed a small child who had survived the butchery. He brought the child home with him, named him Shigikutuku, and brought him up as an adopted son.

Temujin reorganized the traditional Mongol fighting units and developed innovative battle tactics.

With Toghrul as his ally, Temujin was prepared to fight Jamuka, now Gur-Khan (supreme ruler) of a coalition of tribes hostile to Temujin. In around 1201, Jamuka attacked Temujin's and Toghrul's united forces. Before the great battle, a huge rainstorm occurred, so fierce that Jamuka's forces retreated. Once again Temujin and Toghrul were successful.

But the alliance between Temujin and Toghrul had run its course. Like Jamuka and others, Toghrul was afraid of Temujin's growing power, and Jamuka convinced the Kerait chief to join him in a plot to assassinate Temujin. At the time, Temujin was negotiating a marriage for one of his people with one of Toghrul's. At Jamuka's urging, Toghrul invited Temujin to a private dinner to discuss the impending marriage. Temujin set out with only a small escort, but stopped on the way to see a trusted adviser, who warned him of the plot. Temujin sent a messenger to take his place at the dinner and quickly returned to his own camp.

When Toghrul realized that Temujin had learned of the plot, he sent a party of men to find his intended victim. Meanwhile, Temujin had tried to raise some troops but was able to gather only a small band of loyal followers, because the general feeling was that Toghrul would be the victor in this fight, and no one wanted to join the losing side. When Toghrul's and Jamuka's men attacked, Temujin was badly outnumbered and was forced to retreat. But not for long. He regrouped, and attacked Toghrul's camp with six thousand men. The battle lasted for three days and resulted in the total defeat of Toghrul's tribe, the Keraits. Toghrul and his son managed to escape, but they were caught and killed by another tribe.

Temujin proclaimed himself khan of the Keraits in Toghrul's place. He quickly defeated any remaining tribes who opposed him, including Jamuka's. Jamuka was taken prisoner and brought before his former friend and one-time ally. It is said that Jamuka asked only one thing of Temujin. "If, my friend, you are pleased to kill me, do so without shedding my blood."[107] According to most accounts, Temujin honored his request. He had Jamuka wrapped in a carpet and crushed to death with large stones. However, other accounts say Jamuka was executed by dismemberment.

Temujin is warned of Toghrul's and Jamuka's plot to assassinate him.

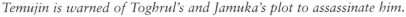

Temujin Becomes Genghis Khan

Temujin was then acknowledged as the first undisputed supreme ruler of the Mongols. By beating his enemies into submission, he had done what no Mongol chieftain had ever done—united the people into one nation. At a grand council of all Mongol tribes in 1206, one of the few dates on which all accounts agree, he was elected as Genghis (perfect warrior) Khan (king).

As ruler, Temujin showed great concern for the welfare of his people. Though he did not accumulate material possessions, he gave them to others as gifts—gold, pearls, clothing. To his bodyguards, a large force of around ten thousand men, he once said, "It is my intention that your wives and daughters shall be dressed from head to foot in gold embroidered dresses, ride quiet geldings and have clean and pleasant tasting water to drink; your herds shall have good pastures and the highways shall be cleared of rubble and rubbish." [108]

He saw to it that all his people were provided for by assessing taxes on the wealthier families to provide felt, for making tents, and sheep's milk cheese to families too poor to supply those things for themselves.

As supreme ruler of all Mongols, Genghis had the responsibilities of administering a growing kingdom. One of the tribes he had conquered was the Naimans, a tribe that had attained a higher degree of civilization than other Mongols, including a written language. From them, Temujin learned "that royal orders should in future be legalized by a seal," and from that time onward he adopted the practice. He also decreed that his top officers learn to read and write, and he and his adopted son, Shigikutuku, devised a set of laws for his people that encompassed everything from rules of conduct in business and private life to what constituted criminal action and what punishments would be handed down for different crimes. He told Shigikutuku to

> Write down the details of the distributions of rewards and of the legal decisions made for the nation and bind these in a Blue Book. Until the days of my most distant successors, no one shall alter whatever, after consultation with myself, what Shigikutuku shall decide and set down in blue writing on white paper. [109]

Genghis then crossed from Mongolia into present-day China, where he spent six years conquering the kingdom of the Tanguts, which lay along the Yellow River. One reason it took so long to subdue these people was their use of weapons unfamiliar to Genghis—flamethrowers, battering rams to break down walls, and catapults.

When the Chinese emperor realized how strong Genghis had become, and that he had a substantial foothold on Chinese territory, he demanded a tribute from him. But Genghis refused to pay the tribute, and instead attacked. Using the new technology copied from the Tanguts, his forces were able to breach the Great Wall of China. China's major cities were laid to waste in bloody battles, and Genghis's armies savagely slaughtered tens of hundreds of people. Accounts record that limbs were chopped off people while they were still alive and small children were skewered onto long lances or piled into great heaps and burned alive while their mothers were forced to watch. In 1215, another date generally agreed on by historians, Genghis and his men conquered the well-fortified capital of China, which at that time was called Zhongdu and today is known as Beijing.

Although Genghis was capable of being cruel and tyrannical, he nonetheless proved himself to be a shrewd and wise military leader. Now, he proved himself a sagacious administrator and leader of conquered peoples as well. For example, he listened when a Chinese official pointed out that if he refrained from destroying everything in his wake and instead allowed conquered people to live, he would reap profits through taxes he could collect. He realized that the Chinese culture was far more advanced than that of the Mongols, and he employed many learned men as counselors. He imposed no restrictions on the way his new subjects carried on their daily lives, nor did he try to prevent them from practicing their religions. In fact, a Taoist monk became one of his teachers and advisers.

While he admired much about the Chinese and learned what he could from them, he never allowed his soldiers to live in China, or in any other place he conquered, because he did not want them to become accustomed to an easy city life. Regardless of how far he took his armies from home, he always maintained his main camp in a remote area in Mongolia, to which he and his men returned after each campaign.

World Conqueror

Once China had been subdued, Genghis reached further afield, but now he sought trade instead of war. He sent ambassadors with a proposal for a trade agreement, along with a caravan of goods, to one of the most powerful rulers in Asia, Sultan Muhammad,

A formidable warrior and effective leader, Genghis Khan amassed an empire reaching from Korea to eastern Europe.

head of the Islamic state of Khwarazm (Persia). The sultan, however, distrusted Genghis's motives and had the ambassadors murdered. When Genghis learned what had happened, he is reported to have "climbed to the top of a hill, bared his head, raised his face to Heaven and prayed to Heaven for three days: 'I was not the instigator of these tribulations. Grant me the strength to exact vengeance!'"[110] And he did exact vengeance. The city of Ortrar, in which the sultan lived, was held under siege for five months. Then, the governor was publicly tortured and every citizen slain. The sultan managed to escape and flee to an island in the Caspian Sea, where he was caught and killed. Genghis's army next plunged through Khwarazm and went on to conquer Samarkand, Afghanistan, part of what is now southern Russia, and other lands that had been under the sultan's control across the Indus River into northern India.

During his long absence in western Asia, the Tanguts rose again in rebellion. Genghis returned to China and led his troops against them, once again defeating them. But during the campaign, he became ill and, fearing he would soon die, called his surviving sons to his side. "My sickness is too serious to cure and one of you will have to defend the throne and the power of the state and expand this structure which has been given such firm foundations."[111] As with so much else in Genghis Khan's life, there are conflicting stories about the circumstances of his death. In one version he became ill as a result of a fall from his horse. Others simply state he became ill. According to another, repeated by Marco Polo, a Venetian who traveled extensively in Asia a generation later, he had been wounded in the knee by an arrow. The only thing sources agree on is that he died in August 1227.

There are conflicting stories, as well, about Temujin's funeral and burial. The official Mongolian records state that he is interred in Mongolia. After his death, his son Ögödei had forty young girls and forty horses sacrificed to his father's spirit.

Genghis Khan's Legacy

Genghis Khan is acknowledged as one of history's greatest military and political leaders. He succeeded in uniting a widely dispersed people into one nation and went on to build an empire that was not only one of the world's greatest, but the first one to truly bridge the worlds of the Far East and the West. The laws he devised remained in effect long after his death and created in Mongolia, for the first time, a place where people could live in relative safety and international trade could flourish. As Ratchnevsky says,

Genghis Khan was the first leader to provide an independent identity for Mongolia and is a national hero to modern Mongolians.

> The achievements of Genghis Khan have disappeared, but their memory remains alive among the Mongolian people. The national consciousness of sharing a common destiny, never completely extinguished among the people despite the struggles which broke out on the steppe after the demise of the empire, has been revived in modern times. From the days of Genghis Khan onwards, Mongolia became Mongolian.[112]

In Mongolia, Genghis Khan is a national hero.

CHAPTER 7

Napoleon Bonaparte: The Little Corporal Who Conquered Europe

The French Revolution began on July 14, 1789, when an angry mob stormed the Bastille prison in Paris. Within a few years the monarchy was dissolved, the king and queen had lost their heads to the guillotine, and the country was declared a republic. Conservative and liberal factions fought for control of the revolutionary government as thousands of other people, no happier with the new regime than they had been under the king, roamed the country rioting and looting. These conditions would lead to a bloody civil war in 1793.

In 1792, however, the fledgling republic turned its aggression outward, declaring war on five European countries that were supporting die-hard French Royalists in their attempt to reinstate the monarchy. That fall, backed by a small fleet of English ships, the Royalists held Toulon, a major port on the southeastern coast of France. The commander in charge of artillery for the revolutionary forces was wounded, and a young officer was assigned as his replacement. Napoleon Buonaparte took control of the situation and, in his first military action, defeated the Royalists and forced the English fleet to flee. No one, least of all Napoleon himself, dreamed that in less than ten years he would be the emperor of France and the conqueror of most of Europe.

Early Years

Napoleon was born August 15, 1768, in Ajaccio, Corsica, a small island between Italy and France. He was the fourth of eight children of Carlo and Letizia Ramolino Buonaparte. Though the Buonapartes were an old and respected Corsican family, they were not wealthy. Carlo was a lawyer, but often he was paid in chickens and eggs instead of cash. The senior Buonaparte wanted his sons to have decent educations, however, and was able to arrange scholarships for them in France.

At the age of ten, Napoleon was sent to a preparatory school, then later to a military academy. From all reports, he was a good student, excelling at mathematics and geography, but he was a quiet, moody boy who spent much of his time alone reading. The other students teased him about his small stature and his Corsican accent. He stood up for himself, though, and was sometimes involved in fights that earned him respect from his fellow students and reprimands from his teachers. Alan Schom, one of Napoleon's many biographers, records that much later, Napoleon said of his school years, "I had even then the belief that my willpower was destined to make me triumph over others."[113]

At fifteen, he won a scholarship to École Militaire in Paris, France's leading military college, where he specialized in the study of artillery. As before, he applied himself to his studies, and he was commissioned as a second lieutenant when he graduated in 1785. The year 1785 brought sorrow as well, however, for Carlo Buonaparte died, and Napoleon stepped in to assume responsibility for the care of his mother and seven brothers and sisters. His lieutenant's salary was small, and he sent most of it to Corsica. In his spare time, he read books on philosophy, classical literature, military history, mathematics, and geography, which he bor-

Napoleon's mother, Letizia Buonaparte.

rowed from the secondhand book shop on the first floor of his apartment house. He was undoubtedly influenced by contemporary eighteenth-century writers like Voltaire and Rousseau, who wrote of man's ability to control his own destiny and individual freedom.

Over the next few years, Napoleon was more concerned with politics in Corsica than events in France. He spent most of his time settling his father's affairs and participating in Corsica's struggle for independence from France. At first he supported Corsica's bid for independence but later reversed his position and worked with those who wanted Corsica to ally with the new French republic. The Corsican people regarded this change as traitorous, however, and Napoleon and his entire family were forced to flee to France in 1793.

Napoleon resumed his position in the French army, which supported the Revolution, was promoted to captain, and tried to support his family on his meager salary. Of Napoleon's activities preceding his public career in France, Schom says, "He realized the chaotic times might provide opportunities, saying, 'Revolutions are ideal times for soldiers with a bit of wit and courage to act.'" Also during this period, Napoleon once said, "The use of brute force is the law of the jungle; the power of reasoning that of man. Tyranny, oppression, and injustice are devastating the earth."[114] Strange words for a man who would impose his own tyranny and oppression on much of Europe.

Napoleon and the French Revolution

Although Napoleon's military debut had been the product of chance—he had been in the right place at the right time at Toulon—the victory of the revolutionary forces over the English was the product of the young artillery commander's ability. This success, in turn, resulted in a promotion to brigadier general and brought Napoleon into contact with Augustin Robespierre, whose brother Maximilien was one of the most powerful leaders of the Revolution.

Carlo Buonaparte, Napoleon's father.

Maximilien Robespierre was in charge of the so-called Reign of Terror during which the government summarily arrested and guillotined thousands of antirevolutionaries and suspected antirevolutionaries. In about a year, however, Maximilien Robespierre fell into disfavor and he and his followers were marched to the guillotine. Because Napoleon had been associated with Augustin Robespierre, he was arrested, but was freed when he was able to convince the new authorities that he was no friend of the architect of the Terror.

Political prisoners during the Reign of Terror, a period of violence and unrest after the French Revolution.

Napoleon was offered a new army post, but he turned it down, becoming a has-been at twenty-five. In desperate need of money, he accepted a job in an office of the new government, where he eked out a living and brooded over his botched career.

However, in October 1795, as Royalist forces threatened to take control of the Tuileries palace in Paris, where the new government had its offices, Napoleon's strong actions at Toulon were recalled, and he was asked to help defend the former royal complex. He agreed on condition that he be given total control, saying "I'll return the sword to its sheath only when everything's finished." He placed heavy cannons in front of the Tuileries and ruthlessly fired into the crowds mobbing the palace. "If it comes to a battle, let it be a victory, come what may; he who thinks of anything but this single aim is lost,"[115] became his motto and his standard of operation from then on.

Rise to Power

Napoleon's actions had saved the revolutionary government. Napoleon was promoted to commander of the Army of the Interior. At this time, he dropped the "u" in his last name to make it more French. He was pleased with the recognition, but rather than fighting antirevolutionaries in France, he wanted to participate in the foreign war against the coalition of European nations that were supporting the Royalists.

Italy and Josephine

Austria, the strongest country of the coalition, controlled northern Italy. Napoleon convinced the government that the best way to defeat Austria was through Italy. Two French armies would invade Italy, one from the south and one from the north, and they would trap the Austrians in the middle. Napoleon was placed in command of the southern army.

His initial elation at the posting faded when he met his troops, a sorry lot in ragged uniforms; some of them lacked even boots. Other troops lacked guns, and no one had been paid in months. Many had deserted, and morale was low. The men were as unhappy with their new commander as he was with them. They had hoped for someone older and more experienced. But Napoleon took things in hand. He imposed strict but fair discipline on the men and demanded new supplies and guns from the government. He told the troops, "You are hungry and naked. The government owes us much but can give us nothing."[116] But he promised them great rewards from the booty they would take from the enemy.

Napoleon was busy with his army, but he also found time to pursue a courtship with a widow he had met earlier that year, Rose de Beauharnais. Madame Beauharnais was well known in the elite social set of Paris and had many other suitors, but she succumbed to Napoleon's frequent letters to her. She told Napoleon, "I awake every day with thoughts only of you."[117] They were married in a civil ceremony on March 6, 1796. Uncomfortable with his bride's past as a courtesan, Napoleon had her change her name to Josephine, hoping that people would forget her former reputation.

Two days after the wedding, Napoleon left to lead his troops over the Alps into Italy, where they won several battles. Summarizing this period, Eugene Tarlé says, "From the first days of his first command Napoleon displayed the most audacious courage and the most utter contempt for personal danger."[118]

Josephine, a Parisian widow, married Napoleon in 1796.

In a victory speech, Napoleon said, "People of Italy! The French Army has just broken your chains of bondage. The French are the friends of all peoples. Have confidence and work with us. Your property, your religion, and your customs will be respected."[119]

But in spite of the words of assurance to the Italians, Napoleon's earlier promise to his own men was fulfilled. They were allowed to plunder and loot and many returned to France wealthy. It was then that adoring troops dubbed their commander "the little corporal."

Napoleon himself acquired much wealth while in Italy and sent millions of dollars in money and treasures home to France. One of the treasures he stole from Italy was *Mona Lisa*, the famous painting by Leonardo da Vinci, which even today hangs in the Louvre museum in Paris. The expedition to Italy officially ended in October 1797, when Napoleon forced the Austrians to surrender and sign the Treaty of Campo Formio, which put not only Austria, but Belgium, the Netherlands, and other territories under French control.

A promotion to commander in chief of the army against England was Napoleon's reward for the victories in Italy. But he was not happy with this. Tarlé reports that he said he wanted to remain in Italy, "where I am more of a sovereign than a general."[120]

He returned to France to a hero's welcome. At twenty-eight he was the most powerful person in France, aside from the members of the Directoire, the five-man committee in charge of the government. Opinions about him in France at this time were mixed. Schom reports that one French general said, "that stunted little man with the uncombed hair, that bastard of a Mandarin . . . will pay for . . . all his boastful glory," and another called him "a new Alexander the Great."[121]

Egyptian Campaign

The revolutionary government instructed Napoleon to plan an invasion of England, but this would have involved a military impossibility: crossing the English Channel in the face of the invincible British Royal Navy. Napoleon pointed out that France could not hope to beat the English at sea and proposed invading Egypt instead. He had earlier written to a friend: "The time is not far distant when we will realize that in order to crush England we must take possession of Egypt."[122] Egypt was the key to the Middle East and to the riches of trade with Asia. Napoleon argued that by controlling Egypt, France would gain control of this lucrative trade and be in a position to cripple England's trade with her colonies in India.

With characteristic bravado, Napoleon convinced the government to change his command and allow him to do what he wanted. Perhaps the men of the Directoire agreed because they were glad to have the ambitious young commander far away from Paris, where he would pose no threat to them.

Napoleon at the Battle of Arcola in Italy in 1796. Though claiming to be liberators, the victorious French looted their newly acquired territory.

Napoleon spent several months preparing his invasion. He had a fleet of ships built, secured arms and supplies, and assembled his troops, many of whom had fought with him in Italy and had proven their loyalty and reliability.

He sailed from France on June 19, 1789, with 350 ships and 30,000 men, including a group of scientists and scholars who would undertake a study of Egypt's antiquities.

Napoleon kept his sailing date and destination secret because he knew that the English admiral, Horatio Nelson, hoped to stop him from reaching Egypt. And, indeed, as soon as Nelson heard that Napoleon had set sail, he set sail also. The two fleets traveled across the Mediterranean Sea, sometimes passing the same point within hours of each other. Nelson thought Napoleon would head for Alexandria, Egypt's main port, and headed there accordingly. But he arrived before Napoleon did, saw no sign of the French fleet, thought he had misjudged, and left.

Within a few hours Napoleon's force landed at Alexandria, and with no opposition, captured the city. Egypt at this time was ruled by Turkey, but it was the Mamelukes, a private cavalry made up of Turkish and Egyptian landowners, who ran the country. Like warlords, the Mamelukes demanded tribute from small farmers and business owners. Using the same approach he had tried in Italy, Napoleon assured the Egyptians he was not at war with them, but was there to liberate them from the Mamelukes. Most Egyptians, however, did not feel liberated. They saw Napoleon as another conqueror who taxed them heavily.

And as had happened in Italy, in spite of his assurances that he meant no harm to Egyptians, Napoleon left almost total devastation in his wake, allowing the army to loot, pillage, and destroy crops on its way south from Alexandria to Cairo. As he led his troops across the desert, he joked that it was too bad he could not proclaim himself a living god, as Alexander the Great had done two thousand years earlier. In some ways he did think of himself as a god, or at least as someone above ordinary law. He once told his staff "I am no longer able to obey."[123]

Napoleon reorganized the government of Egypt. In addition to imposing heavy taxes, he set up a police system, created a health department, and built hospitals for the poor. He also stopped the tributes to the Mamelukes. But his victory was not secure. Many Egyptians opposed him, and the Mamelukes continued to make raids. For all his planning, he could not find important places like granaries because the maps he had brought from France lacked such details. Another indication of inadequate planning was his failure to account for Egypt's incessant heat.

Then, on August 1, 1798, he suffered a blow from which he would not recover. Admiral Nelson came back to Alexandria and in the Battle of Abukir Bay destroyed Napoleon's entire fleet without losing any of his own ships.

The Battle at Abukir Bay in 1798 was a devastating loss for Napoleon.

Napoleon was not at Alexandria at the time of Nelson's victory, and now his army was trapped in Egypt with no way to get home. The French were also cut off from any news from Europe. He decided to make his way out of Egypt over land, taking his army first through Syria, which he conquered, and then to Palestine, which today is Israel. When his troops reached the walled city of Acre (now Akko), they were met by a strong force of English and Turks. At this point, lacking the equipment he needed to breach Acre's walls, his troops exhausted and ill, Napoleon was forced to retreat.

On the way back across the desert to Cairo, hundreds of men died from illness, heat exhaustion, and thirst. Napoleon showed himself to be compassionate by sharing their hardships, marching with them on foot, and leaving wagon transport for those too ill to march.

In Egypt, he finally received news from France, and it was not good. The European coalition he had defeated in Italy had reformed and was again fighting against France. Within France new riots and revolts had erupted against the government. Napoleon declared, "The wretches! Italy lost! All the fruits of victory lost! I must go!"[124]

Napoleon knew his army in Egypt was doomed, and rather than remain in a hopeless situation, he left the expeditionary forces in charge of another general and returned to France, claiming in his reports, "I have left Egypt well organized."[125] Two years later, the remnants of Napoleon's army in Egypt surrendered to the English.

Napoleon's Coup

Napoleon arrived in France in October 1799. The country was again in chaos. The treasury was bankrupt. People were rioting for food. As had occurred so many times over the past several years, various factions and individuals were vying for control of the government.

One politician, a former priest named Emmanuel Sieyès, enlisted Napoleon's help, thinking that he would lead the government, with Napoleon as his military commander. Napoleon had other ideas. While seeming to go along with Sieyès, Napoleon contrived to have himself appointed as commander of all troops around Paris and made secret plans for his own account.

Working closely with Sieyès, his brother Lucien Bonaparte, who had become influential in the government, and other trusted friends, Napoleon orchestrated his takeover of the government.

To justify the coup, he made an inflammatory speech to a low-level government functionary in the presence of army troops intensely loyal to himself: "What have you done with the France which I left you in such a brilliant state? I left you peace; I find war! I left you victories; I find defeats! I left you the Italian millions; I find pillaging laws and poverty! What have you done with the hundred thousand Frenchmen whom I knew, comrades in my glory? They are dead!"[126]

Napoleon's coup, on November 18 and 19, 1799, marked the end of the Revolution. He formed a new government made up of three consuls and two legislative bodies. On December 24, Napoleon was officially sworn in as first consul. The other two consuls, like the legislatures, were nothing more than window dressing to lend the appearance of a democratic process to what had become a dictatorship.

Napoleon accomplished his coup in 1799.

The little boy who left Corsica at ten years old was, at the age of thirty, the ruler of France. Tarlé says, "In all his political undertakings, Napoleon's ultimate purpose was to establish and consolidate his complete supremacy."[127]

Napoleon's Government

Once in power, Napoleon set about reorganizing, not only the French government, but nearly all aspects of life in France. To protect himself from opposition he closed most newspapers and imposed strict censorship on the rest. He created a Ministry of Justice and a Ministry of Police. One segment of the police was used to spy on anyone he suspected of being a danger to him or his government, but the main force set about enforcing strict new laws and rounding up the many roving bands of criminals who were terrorizing the countryside. Tarlé describes Napoleon's philosophy as follows: "it was better to punish ten innocent people than to allow a single guilty person to escape."[128]

Many major changes had been initiated by revolutionary governments over the past ten years, but they were solidified and made permanent under Napoleon. He refined property and tax laws, making them fairer. He enforced laws that encouraged people to own and run businesses. He stabilized the economy and balanced the budget. Among some of the most important changes he instituted were in France's financial, judicial, and educational systems.

He completely reorganized and centralized France's financial system under the Bank of France, a giant economic bureaucracy that regulated all currency, public loans, and foreign and domestic trade.

Before Napoleon took over, France's legal system consisted of a quagmire of nearly four hundred separate legal codes in different areas and municipalities. What was a crime in one place was perfectly legal in another. Even when a particular activity was judged a crime in several places, the punishments differed—in one place an offense might bring only a fine, whereas in another the penalty for the same crime would be an extended prison sentence.

Napoleon dictates to his secretaries. Napoleon introduced many reforms to the French financial, educational, and legal systems.

Under Napoleon's direction, experts devised the Napoleonic Code of Law, a new unified system of civil, commercial, and criminal law for the entire country. Napoleon's Code made all French citizens equal under the law and provided the rights of habeas corpus (protection against illegal arrest and detainment) and legal representation.

Napoleon's Code was stern and often harsh. Business owners and farmers had rights over their employees. Husbands had total control of their wives, and fathers had total rule over their children. Women's rights were practically nonexistent. One writer attributed to Napoleon the opinion that women should be taught "to believe, not to think."[129] Illegitimate children had no rights, nor could they inherit from their fathers. This law was to affect Napoleon's own two illegitimate sons: one immigrated to the United States, where he became a cook, and the other became active in French politics, but neither inherited anything from Napoleon's estate. Divorce, once outlawed in France because of the influence of the Catholic Church, had been made easily available during the Revolution. Napoleon did not restore the ban on divorce but made it more difficult to obtain.

But along with its harshness and biases, the new laws did grant rights to French citizens they had not formerly had. Most important among these were the guarantee of religious freedom, the right of all citizens to a fair trial, and the right of peasants to purchase land.

Years later, when Napoleon had lost his empire, he said the world would remember his defeats more than his victories, but "That which can never be denied, and that [which] will live on forever, is my Civil Code."[130] The Napoleonic Code is still the basis of law not only in France, but in Belgium, Holland, Italy, some South American countries, and the state of Louisiana. He also established a comprehensive educational system, still used in France, that oversees everything from primary schools to universities.

Napoleon reestablished official relations between his government, the Catholic Church in France, and the pope in Rome. However, the amount of land the church could own and the appointments of bishops were strictly regulated by the French government.

Not all these changes were completed at once, but within a few months of his leadership the civil war that had been tearing the country apart had been stopped, the worst of the criminals had been apprehended, and the country was quite well stabilized.

War Again

Napoleon knew that the European monarchists were re-forming their coalition and preparing for another war, still hoping to restore a member of the executed king's family to the throne of France. Leaving the government in charge of a trusted subordinate, Napoleon donned his general's uniform and led his army across the Alps, where he defeated the Austrians at Marengo and forced them to sign a treaty that placed Italy under French control. He also fought sea battles with England and won a temporary peace with his island neighbor. But within less than a year, he was at war again, this time with several other European countries who had again re-formed the coalition. War continued for several more years, especially with England, one of Napoleon's primary enemies, and one whom he would dearly have loved to conquer.

Napoleon became a popular dictator. Under his rule, revolution was finally ended. He had also established France as an important power, regaining several of the territories lost during the time he was in Egypt. When he had established his government, the consulship he manufactured for himself was to have run for ten years, but in 1802 he proposed that this be changed to a lifetime office. To no one's surprise, his tame legislatures voted almost unanimously to award him this honor.

Emperor of France and Conqueror of Europe

On December 2, 1804, there was in Paris one of the grandest celebrations in Europe in centuries. Troops in full dress uniform lined

A charismatic leader, Napoleon earned the genuine respect and whole-hearted support of his soldiers.

the streets. Thousands of people were massed—not to riot, but to watch the grand procession of carriages pouring into the city from all of France. The carriages were filled with the new elite of French society and dignitaries from several foreign countries. Even the pope was there with his full retinue. Over eight thousand people pushed themselves into Notre Dame Cathedral to await the anticipated ceremony.

Finally, Napoleon's glass-paneled carriage, lavishly decorated with a large golden "N" entwined with laurel leaves, arrived. The carriage was drawn by eight matched stallions with braided manes adorned with red and gold ribbons. Royalty had returned to France. Napoleon had declared himself emperor and this was his coronation. Displaying his typical arrogance, he had even placed the crown on his own head instead of allowing the pope to bestow this honor upon him. In the continued charade of making his dictatorship appear to be part of a democratic process, there had been a public vote: 3,572,329 in favor of making France an empire; 2,569 against the proposal.

Aside from the personal satisfaction Napoleon gained from his new position, being emperor gave him the right to hand his rule on to his son. The only problem was that he had no legitimate son. Though he truly loved Josephine, when it became apparent she would have no more children, Napoleon divorced her to

On December 2, 1804, Napoleon rode in this ornate carriage through the streets of Paris to Notre Dame Cathedral for his coronation.

marry Marie-Louise, the eighteen-year-old daughter of the emperor of Austria, who had many childbearing years ahead of her.

With his position thus secure in France, Napoleon was determined to conquer his enemies and add their domains to his empire. He planned to invade England, but before he got the chance England's great admiral Horatio Nelson once again destroyed the French fleet, this time in the Battle of Trafalgar near the southwestern tip of Spain. And just as had happened in Egypt, not a single English ship was lost, although Lord Nelson was fatally wounded.

Swallowing his defeat, Napoleon turned his attention to the rest of Europe and over the next seven years conquered most of it. At that time, the territory now forming Germany was a collection of small states. Napoleon combined many of these into the Confederation of the Rhine. He installed his brothers as kings of several countries and arranged royal marriages for his sisters.

But he was still obsessed with destroying England. Once before he had tried to cripple England by interfering with her trade in the Middle East. In 1807 he tried yet again, ordering that no European ports could trade with England. And although by 1814 he was the most powerful ruler in Europe, with an empire that extended from France almost to Russia, the few places he did not control refused to honor the blockade.

Reaching Too Far: Russian Defeat

Although Russia had signed a treaty with France agreeing not to trade with England, the agreement was ignored. In February 1811, Napoleon wrote to the czar, "Your Majesty's last ukase [proclamation] both in essence and form was specifically directed against France, and therefore . . . our alliance no longer exists."[131] Napoleon had already decided to go to war against Russia, and the country's noncompliance with France's blockade provided him with the excuse he needed. Meanwhile, Czar Alexander, well aware of Napoleon's ambition to control all of Europe, was also mobilizing for war. He secretly told the deposed rulers of the other European countries, "I am sick and tired of Napoleon's continued meddling in our affairs. I have 200,000 good troops ready, and another 300,000 in my militia, with which to challenge him, and we shall then see."[132] The czar knew if he could entice Napoleon onto Russian territory, he stood a good chance of winning.

Napoleon amassed a huge army and set out to cross Europe in May 1812, leaving his new wife and the son to whom she had recently given birth in Paris. Most of the way the emperor rode in a special carriage large enough to hold a folding bed, a wash basin, a desk, and a bookcase. He crossed the Russian border in June, only to find that the Russian army had retreated into the interior. Napoleon had no choice but to pursue them. He reached Moscow on September 15, but found the city deserted. He was impressed with the beauty of the Kremlin, Russia's seat of government, but not impressed enough to keep his men from looting many Russian treasures. That night the city erupted in fires. Napoleon found and executed a few Russian soldiers he claimed were responsible, but some historians suggest that the fires were set by Napoleon's men. At any rate, the flames had destroyed food and supplies desper-

Napoleon's Empire, 1799–1812

NORWAY
SWEDEN
Stockholm
Moscow
DENMARK
North Sea
UNITED KINGDOM OF GREAT BRITAIN AND IRELAND
London
RUSSIA
Berlin
Warsaw
GRAND DUCHY OF WARSAW
English Channel
CONFEDERATION OF THE RHINE 1806
Atlantic Ocean
Paris
FRANCE
AUSTRIA
Vienna
Bay of Biscay
SWITZERLAND
ITALY
Black Sea
PORTUGAL
Elba
PAPAL STATES
Adriatic Sea
OTTOMAN EMPIRE
Constantinople
Madrid
Corsica
Rome
SPAIN
Naples
Sardinia
Tyrrhenian Sea
Aegean Sea
Cyprus

France, 1799
Under French Rule by 1812
Allied with France in 1812

Sicily
Mediterranean Sea
Crete
Alexandria
EGYPT
Cairo

ately needed by the exhausted French troops. By the beginning of October, Napoleon ordered a retreat. But an early winter attacked his unprepared troops, who had only lightweight uniforms. Thousands of soldiers froze to death as they tramped in icy temperatures through the deep snow. Only a very small portion of Napoleon's vast army survived what had turned into a veritable death march. The Russian war was a total disaster.

Napoleon's Decline

More disaster was to follow. In the wake of his Russian defeat, the European coalition re-formed and rebelled against his rule. Even the Austrians turned against him, despite his being married to Marie-Louise, their emperor's daughter. In 1813 the combined European forces invaded France and occupied Paris. Napoleon's empire was in shambles. Within France, he was no longer a hero, but the man who had led the nation to ruin. His once tame legislative bodies revolted against him, demanding the end of the empire and a new constitution guaranteeing true freedom.

On April 11, 1814, Napoleon abdicated his throne and was exiled to Elba, a small island off the coast of Italy. Considering his position, the terms of his banishment from France were mild. Although his wife and son were not allowed to accompany him, he was awarded a generous pension and given command of the island.

Defeated French troops retreat from Moscow in the bitter cold.

Before he left he wrote a final letter of farewell to Marie-Louise who, with their son, would go back to Austria to live with her father. He also wrote a final letter to Josephine, whom he still loved; the former empress would die of pneumonia a month later.

Napoleon was so despondent that he took the poison he always carried with him in case of capture by enemies. But even in this he was not successful. The drug had lost its potency, and although he was quite ill, he did not die. Instead, he departed for Elba on April 27, 1814.

On May 3, the French people cheered at the coronation of King Louis XVIII, the brother of Louis XVI, the king who had been guillotined. (The son of Louis XVI, also named Louis, died in prison during the Revolution.) But Napoleon was not idle on Elba. He kept in close contact with certain friends, and when he heard that Louis was losing his initial popularity and the country was again in chaos, he plotted his return.

He clandestinely left Elba and landed in France on March 1, 1815, with around a thousand men, and began his march to Paris. Still popular with many of the people, he gathered more troops along the way. At one point, he was stopped by the king's army. Instead of submitting, he said to them, "Soldiers of the 5th Infantry Regiment, I am your Emperor. If there is any one among you who wishes to kill his emperor, here I am," and he boldly opened his coat exposing his chest. No one fired. The soldiers put down their guns and cheered him with cries of "Vive l'Empereur [life to the emperor]!"[133]

On March 20, Napoleon was back in Paris and easily retook the government. Louis fled for his life. Napoleon maintained his new government for one hundred days. Once again he prepared to battle the European coalition, and once again, he went to meet the enemy instead of waiting for them to come to him. He met the coalition forces in Belgium in a small town called Waterloo. This was to be his final battle. He was soundly defeated by a combined English/Prussian attack.

Napoleon returned to France in disgrace and attempted unsuccessfully to arrange a secret passage to America. He was taken to England, tried, and exiled to another island, to St. Helena, a tiny, insignificant dot of land seven hundred miles off the coast of West Africa.

He lived there, isolated from all he had known, for the rest of his days. For many years official records stated that his death, in 1821, was due to a natural stomach ailment, but there had al-ways been rumors that he had been poisoned. During the 1990s, DNA tests applied to the former emperor's remains proved those rumors to be true. His death was slow and painful, the result of a combination of arsenic and cyanide fed to him by his doctors who hoped to profit from his death. They did not.

Napoleon was given a full state funeral with two thousand full-dress English troops in attendance. He was laid to rest in a crypt on St. Helena. In his will, Napoleon had asked to be buried near the Seine River in Paris. His body was returned to France in 1840.

Napoleon abdicated in 1814 and was exiled to Elba.

The twice-exiled emperor spent his last days on the island of St. Helena.

Legacy

Napoleon Bonaparte was undoubtedly one of history's greatest military geniuses, renowned for courageously leading his men in battle, something most generals at that time avoided. He evoked fierce loyalty from followers and was a superb administrator, but he refused to delegate responsibility. He is praised for his law code and for other improvements in the public institutions of France, many of which are the basis of today's systems. Many historians believe that his changes to the map of Europe continue to influence modern history.

But he made a farce of the ideas of democracy, allowing no freedom of the press and employing a strong secret police to enforce his tyranny. Hundreds of thousands died because of Napoleon and much of Europe was destroyed. His overriding ambition and compulsion to place himself at the pinnacle of power, combined with an abundance of what the ancient Greeks called hubris, was his ultimate downfall.

NOTES

Chapter 1: Two Thousand Years of Conquerors

1. James Breasted, *The Conquest of Civilization*. Edited by Edith Williams Ware. New York: Harper & Brothers, 1938, p. 419.

2. David Stockton, "The Founding of the Empire," in John Boardman, Jasper Griffen, and Oswyn Murray, eds., *The Oxford History of the Classical World*. New York: Oxford University Press, 1992, p. 539.

3. Patrick Howarth, *Attila, King of the Huns: Man and Myth*. Carlisle, PA: John Kallman, 1994, p. 17.

4. Quoted in Richard Winston, *Charlemagne*. New York: Harper & Row, 1968, p. 52.

5. Quoted in *Bullfinch's Mythology*. Middlesex, England: Hamlyn, 1931, p. 529.

6. Eugene Tarlé, *Bonaparte*. New York: Knight Publications, 1937, p. 89.

7. Edward Ashcroft, "Napoleon Bonaparte," in John Canning, ed., *100 Great Kings, Queens, and Rulers of the World*. New York: Taplinger, 1967, p. 536.

Chapter 2: Alexander the Great: Founder of the Hellenistic Age

8. Breasted, *The Conquest of Civilization*, p. 419.

9. Plutarch, *The Age of Alexander: Nine Greek Lives*. Translated by Ian Scott-Kilvert. New York: Penguin Books, 1973, p. 256.

10. Jack M. Balcer, "Alexander the Great," in *McGraw-Hill Encyclopedia of World Biography*. New York: McGraw-Hill, 1973, p. 121.

11. Quoted in Will Durant, *The Story of Civilization*, vol. II, *The Life of Greece*. New York: Simon & Schuster, 1966, p. 538.

12. Breasted, *The Conquest of Civilization*, p. 407.

13. Quoted in Gail Stewart, *The Importance of Alexander the Great*. San Diego: Lucent Books, 1994, p. 22.

14. Plutarch (Scott-Kilvert), p. 257.

15. Plutarch (Scott-Kilvert), p. 258.

16. Plutarch (Scott-Kilvert), p. 260.

17. Quoted in John Popovic, *Alexander the Great,* Alexandros III Philippou Makedonon, Alexander III of Macedon (356–323 BCE). Project by John J. Popovic, www.1stmuse.com/frames.

18. Plutarch (Scott-Kilvert), p. 261.

19. Plutarch (Scott-Kilvert), p. 263.

20. Quoted in Mary Renault, *The Nature of Alexander.* New York: Pantheon Books, 1975, p. 80.

21. Plutarch, *Plutarch's Lives.* Selected and edited by John S. White. New York: Tannen, 1966, p. 418.

22. Plutarch (Scott-Kilvert), p. 266.

23. Arrian, *The Campaigns of Alexander.* Translated by Aubrey De Sélincourt. New York: Penguin Books, 1958, p. 66.

24. Plutarch (White), p. 431.

25. Plutarch (White), p. 435.

26. Quoted in Popovic, *Alexander the Great.*

27. Renault, *The Nature of Alexander,* p. 110.

28. Plutarch (Scott-Kilvert), p. 284.

29. Breasted, *The Conquest of Civilization,* p. 414.

30. Renault, *The Nature of Alexander,* p. 125.

31. Plutarch (White), p. 437.

32. Durant, *The Life of Greece,* p. 546.

33. Alexander of Macedon Temple. www.sangha.net/messengers/alex.htm.

34. Quoted in Renault, *The Nature of Alexander,* p. 231.

Chapter 3: Augustus the Great: First Roman Emperor

35. Nicolaus of Damascus, excerpts from *Life of Augustus.* Translated by Clayton M. Hall, 1923. www.csun.edu/~hcfll004/nicolaus.html.

36. Michael Grant, *The Roman Emperors: A Biographical Guide to the Rulers of Imperial Rome, 31 BC–AD 476.* New York: Charles Scribner's Sons, 1985, p. 15.

37. Nicolaus, *Life of Augustus.*

38. Nicolaus, *Life of Augustus.*

39. Suetonius, *Lives of the Twelve Caesars,* published as *The Twelve Caesars.* Translated by Robert Graves. New York: Penguin Books, 1979, p. 57.

40. Breasted, *The Conquest of Civilization*, p. 553.

41. Henry T. Rowell, *Rome in the Augustan Age.* Tulsa: University of Oklahoma Press, 1962, pp. 16–17.

42. Letter 14, 12, April 22, 44 B.C., in Cicero, *Letters to Atticus,* vol. 3. Translated and edited by D. R. Shackleton Bailey. Cambridge, MA: Harvard University Press, 1999, p. 241.

43. Suetonius, *The Twelve Caesars*, p. 67.

44. Michael Grant, *The World of Rome.* New York: World Publishing, 1960, p. 12.

45. Breasted, *The Conquest of Civilization*, p. 554.

46. Breasted, *The Conquest of Civilization*, p. 560.

47. Quoted in Suetonius, *The Twelve Caesars*, p. 69.

48. Tacitus, *Annals*, published as *Tacitus: The Annals of Imperial Rome*. Translated by Michael Grant. New York: Penguin Books, 1989, p. 32.

49. Suetonius, *The Twelve Caesars*, p. 68.

50. Suetonius, *The Twelve Caesars*, p. 67.

51. Quoted in Suetonius, *The Twelve Caesars*, p. 69.

52. Virgil, *Aeneid*, Book VI.ii. Internet Ancient History Sourcebook. www.fordham.edu/halsall/ancient/augustanencomions.html.

53. Quoted in Chris Scarre, *Chronicle of the Roman Emperors, the Reign-by-Reign Record of the Rulers of Imperial Rome.* London: Thames & Hudson, 1995, p. 24.

54. Quoted in Suetonius, *The Twelve Caesars*, p. 110.

55. Quoted in Michael Witoski, "Augustus," *Great Lives from History*, Vol. 1. Pasadena, CA: Salem Press, 1998, p. 289.

Chapter 4: Attila: King of the Huns

56. Quoted in Howarth, *Attila, King of the Huns*, p. 161.

57. Quoted in Attila website. http://art1.candor.com/barbarian/attila.htm#Hun.

58. Quoted in Howarth, *Attila, King of the Huns*, p. 16.

59. Quoted in Howarth, *Attila, King of the Huns*, p. 18.

60. Quoted in Howarth, *Attila, King of the Huns*, p. 20.

61. Howarth, *Attila, King of the Huns*, p. 20.

62. Quoted in Attila website.

63. H. L. Oerter, "Attila," in Anne Commire, ed., *Historic World Leaders,* vol. 2. Detroit: Gale Research, 1994, p. 62.

64. Quoted in Steven Béla Vardy, *Attila.* New York: Chelsea House, 1991, p. 13.

65. Quoted in Vardy, *Attila,* p. 47.

66. Quoted in Vardy, *Attila,* p. 47.

67. Quoted in Howarth, *Attila, King of the Huns,* p. 49.

68. Quoted in Howarth, *Attila, King of the Huns,* pp. 73–74.

69. Quoted in Howarth, *Attila, King of the Huns,* pp. 73–74.

70. Quoted in Howarth, *Attila, King of the Huns,* p. 112.

71. Quoted in Howarth, *Attila, King of the Huns,* p. 111.

72. Quoted in Howarth, *Attila, King of the Huns,* p. 113.

73. Howarth, *Attila, King of the Huns,* p. 45.

74. Quoted in C. D. Gordon, *The Age of Attila: Fifth Century Byzantium and the Barbarians.* Ann Arbor: University of Michigan Press, 1969, p. 110.

75. Howarth, *Attila, King of the Huns,* p. 138.

76. Quoted in Howarth, *Attila, King of the Huns,* p. 139.

Chapter 5: Charlemagne: First Holy Roman Emperor

77. Winston, *Charlemagne,* p. 115.

78. J. Kelley Sowards, ed., *Makers of the Western Tradition: Portraits from History,* vol. 1. New York: St. Martin's Press, 1991, p. 116.

79. Einhard, *The Life of Charlemagne.* Ann Arbor: University of Michigan Press, 1960, p. 24.

80. Quoted in Donald Bullough, *The Age of Charlemagne,* 2nd ed. London: Paul Elek, 1973, p. 40.

81. Einhard, *The Life of Charlemagne,* p. 54.

82. Einhard, *The Life of Charlemagne,* p. 54.

83. Quoted in Richard Winston, *Charlemagne: From Hammer to Cross.* New York: Random House, 1954, p. 42.

84. Winston, *Charlemagne,* p. 56.

85. Einhard and Notker the Stammerer, *Two Lives of Charlemagne.* Translated by Lewis Thorpe. New York: Penguin Books, 1969, p. 75.

86. Einhard and Notker, *Two Lives of Charlemagne,* p. 75.

87. Quoted in Sowards, *Makers of the Western Tradition*, p. 122.

88. Winston, *Charlemagne*, p. 68.

89. Einhard and Notker, *Two Lives of Charlemagne*, p. 67.

90. Einhard and Notker, *Two Lives of Charlemagne*, p. 129.

91. Quoted in Susan Banfield, *Charlemagne*. New York: Chelsea House, 1986, p. 65.

92. Bullough, *The Age of Charlemagne*, p. 79.

93. Quoted in Russell Andrew McDonald, "Charlemagne," in *Historic World Leaders*, vol. 2, p. 205.

94. Einhard and Notker, *Two Lives of Charlemagne*, p. 76.

95. Winston, *Charlemagne: From Hammer to Cross*, p. v.

Chapter 6: Genghis Khan: Supreme Ruler of All Mongols

96. Quoted in Paul Ratchnevsky, *Genghis Khan, His Life and Legacy*. Cambridge, MA: Blackwell Publishers, 1991, p. 28.

97. Quoted in Karen Waller, "Genghis Khan," in *Historic World Leaders*, vol. 1, p. 177.

98. Ratchnevsky, *Genghis Khan*, p. 154.

99. Quoted in Ratchnevsky, *Genghis Khan*, p. 21.

100. Quoted in Ratchnevsky, *Genghis Khan*, p. 23.

101. Quoted in Ratchnevsky, *Genghis Khan*, p. 26.

102. Quoted in Ratchnevsky, *Genghis Khan*, p. 33.

103. Quoted in Ratchnevsky, *Genghis Khan*, p. 33.

104. Quoted in Ratchnevsky, *Genghis Khan*, p. 35.

105. Quoted in Ratchnevsky, *Genghis Khan*, pp. 40, 41.

106. Quoted in Ratchnevsky, *Genghis Khan*, p. 151.

107. Quoted in Ratchnevsky, *Genghis Khan*, p. 88.

108. Quoted in Ratchnevsky, *Genghis Khan*, p. 148.

109. Quoted in Ratchnevsky, *Genghis Khan*, pp. 94, 95.

110. Quoted in Ratchnevsky, *Genghis Khan*, p. 123.

111. Quoted in Ratchnevsky, *Genghis Khan*, p. 141.

112. Ratchnevsky, *Genghis Khan*, p. 213.

Chapter 7: Napoleon Bonaparte: The Little Corporal Who Conquered Europe

113. Quoted in Alan Schom, *Napoleon Bonaparte*, New York: HarperCollins, 1997, p. 4.

114. Quoted in Schom, *Napoleon Bonaparte,* pp. 11, 12.

115. Quoted in Tarlé, *Bonaparte,* pp. 31, 32.

116. Quoted in Schom, *Napoleon Bonaparte,* p. 42.

117. Quoted in Schom, *Napoleon Bonaparte,* p. 35.

118. Tarlé, *Bonaparte,* p. 39.

119. Quoted in Schom, *Napoleon Bonaparte,* p. 47.

120. Quoted in Tarlé, *Bonaparte,* p. 56.

121. Quoted in Schom, *Napoleon Bonaparte,* p. 60.

122. Quoted in Tarlé, *Bonaparte,* p. 59.

123. Quoted in Tarlé, *Bonaparte,* p. 60.

124. Quoted in Tarlé, *Bonaparte,* p. 71.

125. Quoted in Schom, *Napoleon Bonaparte,* p. 187.

126. Quoted in Tarlé, *Bonaparte,* p. 82.

127. Tarlé, *Bonaparte,* p. 89.

128. Tarlé, *Bonaparte,* p. 95.

129. Ashcroft, "Napoleon Bonaparte," p. 536.

130. Quoted in Schom, *Napoleon Bonaparte,* p. 293.

131. Quoted in Schom, *Napoleon Bonaparte,* p. 584.

132. Quoted in Schom, *Napoleon Bonaparte,* p. 584.

133. Quoted in Schom, *Napoleon Bonaparte,* p. 712.

FOR FURTHER READING

Paul J. Alexander, ed., *The Ancient World: To 300 AD*. New York: Macmillan, 1963. A collection of ancient Greek and Roman writings, including Augustus's *Res gestae*.

Isaac Asimov, *The Greeks: A Great Civilization*. Boston: Houghton Mifflin, 1965. An older book, but contains excellent historical background.

———, *The Roman Empire*. Boston: Houghton Mifflin, 1967. Good overview of the period. Easy reading.

Susan Banfield, *Charlemagne*. New York: Chelsea House, 1986. Well-written and interesting biography for young adults. Contains much useful information and many insights into Charlemagne's world.

Alan Blackwood, *Napoleon*. New York: Bookwright Press, 1987. Easy to read. Illustrated. A general overview of Napoleon's career.

Bob Carroll, *The Importance of Napoleon Bonaparte*. San Diego: Lucent Books, 1994. A well-researched, lively biography focusing on the highlights of Napoleon's life, his accomplishments, and their significance.

Owen Connelly, ed., *Historical Dictionary of Napoleonic France, 1799–1815*. Westport, CT: Greenwood Press, 1985. Good for basic reference.

Trevor Nevitt Dupuy, *The Military Life of Alexander the Great of Macedon*. New York: Franklin Watts, 1969. Contains detailed descriptions of major battles and discussions of Alexander's military strategies.

John B. Firth, *Augustus Caesar and the Organization of the Empire of Rome*. Freeport, NY: Books for the Libraries Press, 1972. Includes a section on Augustus's rise to power.

Robert Fossier, *Cambridge Illustrated History of the Middle Ages*. New York: Guild Publishing, 1989. Good general reference.

Michael Grant, *The Twelve Caesars*. New York: Charles Scribner's Sons, 1983. Profiles based on translations of Suetonius.

N. G. L. Hammond, *Alexander the Great: King, Commander, and Statesman*. Park Ridge, NJ: Noyes Press, 1980. Somewhat difficult reading, but contains good details of Alexander's military life.

G. Holmes, ed., *The Oxford Illustrated History of Medieval Europe*. New York: Oxford University Press, 1988. A good general reference.

Judy Humphrey, *Genghis Khan*. New York: Chelsea House, 1987. A good examination of Genghis Khan's life.

Lawrence Keppie, *The Making of the Roman Army*. New York: Barnes & Noble, 1994. Good source for students interested in military history.

Stephen Krensky, *Conqueror and Hero: The Search for Alexander*. Boston: Little, Brown, 1981. A good account of Alexander's early years. Easy reading.

Anthony Marks and Graham Tingay, *The Romans*. London: Usborne, 1990. Easy reading. Good for younger readers.

Albert Marrin, *Napoleon and the Napoleonic Wars*. New York: Viking, 1991. Napoleon's life with a focus on his military career.

Allan Massie, *The Caesars*. New York: Franklin Watts, 1984. Includes a good profile of Alexander.

Don Nardo, *The Age of Augustus*. San Diego: Lucent Books, 1996. More than a biography, this book examines the time in which Augustus lived.

————, *Rulers of Ancient Rome*. San Diego: Lucent Books, 1999. A volume in this series. Includes a good, short biography of Augustus emphasizing his role as ruler of the Roman Empire.

Henry T. Rowell, *Rome in the Augustan Age*. Norman: University of Oklahoma Press, 1962. Long considered a basic text on this period of history.

Desmond Seward, *Napoleon and Hitler*. New York: Viking, 1989. For serious readers interested in world history.

Chester G. Starr, *The Ancient Romans*. New York: Oxford University Press, 1971. Good research source as it contains several quotes from Roman and Greek writers.

Gail B. Stewart, *The Importance of Alexander the Great*. San Diego: Lucent Books, 1994. Excellent full biography showing Alexander's development and personality as well as his military accomplishments. Includes background on Macedonian, Greek, and Persian history.

Jakob Walter, *The Diary of a Napoleonic Foot Soldier*. Garden City, NY: Doubleday, 1991. Diary of a teenage soldier in Napoleon's army.

Nancy Zinsser Walworth, *Augustus Caesar*. New York: Chelsea House, 1987. A well-researched full biography of Augustus with extensive historical background.

Albert Wass, ed., *Selected Hungarian Legends*. Astor Park, FL: Danubian Press, 1971. A glimpse at the Hungarian view of Attila.

Ben Weider, *The Murder of Napoleon*. New York: Congdon & Latters. Distributed by St. Martin's Press, 1982. Presents evidence that Napoleon was murdered.

Major Works Consulted

Ancient Sources

Arrian, *The Campaigns of Alexander*. Translated by Aubrey De Sélincourt. New York: Penguin Books, 1958. This biography, as indicated by the title, focuses on Alexander's military accomplishments. Arrian, whose full name was Flavius Arrianus, was a Greek historian who lived from about 95 to 180.

Cicero, *Letters to Atticus*. 4 vols. Translated and edited by D. R. Shackleton Bailey. Cambridge, MA: Harvard University Press, 1999. Cicero's letters give a firsthand look at ancient Romans.

Dio Cassius, *The Roman History: The Reign of Augustus*. Translated by Ian Scott-Kilvert. New York: Penguin Books, 1987. A good source for primary material.

Einhard and Notker the Stammerer, *Two Lives of Charlemagne*. Translated by Lewis Thorpe. New York: Penguin Books, 1969. A look at Charlemagne from the eyes of two men who lived at the same time he did.

Einhard, *The Life of Charlemagne*. Ann Arbor: University of Michigan Press, 1960. Different edition of *Two Lives of Charlemagne*.

Plutarch, *The Age of Alexander: Nine Greek Lives*. Translated by Ian Scott-Kilvert. New York: Penguin Books, 1973. An excellent translation of the original Greek in contemporary language style. Plutarch (ca. 46–120) was a Greek biographer and essayist regarded in his own time as a teacher, philosopher, and spiritual director. His *Parallel Lives* consists of biographies of eight famous Greeks and Romans. Much of what is known today of these men comes from the writings of Plutarch.

———, *Plutarch's Lives*. Selected and edited by John S. White. New York: Tannen, 1966. White's selections were originally translated by John Dryden. This book is written in a more pedantic style than Scott-Kilvert's.

Suetonius, *Lives of the Twelve Caesars*, published as *The Twelve Caesars*. Translated by Robert Graves. New York: Penguin Books, 1979. Suetonius was a Roman historian and biographer. The section on Augustus contains many of his personal opinions and observations.

Tacitus, *Annals*, published as *Tacitus: The Annals of Imperial Rome*. Translated by Michael Grant. New York: Penguin Books, 1989. Tacitus was a Roman general and historian. His account focuses on the military aspects of Augustus's career.

Modern Sources

John Boardman, Jasper Griffen, and Oswyn Murray, eds., *The Oxford History of the Classical World*. New York: Oxford University Press, 1992. Good general reference.

James Breasted, *The Conquest of Civilization*. Edited by Edith Williams Ware. New York: Harper & Brothers, 1938. A classic text on ancient history.

Donald Bullough, *The Age of Charlemagne*. 2nd ed. London: Paul Elek, 1973. Good basic information, but the real value of this book lies in the wonderful color plates and excellent photographs of places and items relating to Charlemagne and his world.

Will Durant, *The Story of Civilization*, Vol. II, *The Life of Greece*. New York: Simon & Schuster, 1966. A classic text on ancient history. Contains chapters or mentions of Alexander and Augustus.

C. D. Gordon, *The Age of Attila: Fifth Century Byzantium and the Barbarians*. Ann Arbor: University of Michigan Press, 1969. A basic translation of excerpts from primary sources on Attila. Difficult to use, but a useful resource to use in conjunction with other materials. For the serious student.

Michael Grant, *The Roman Emperors: A Biographical Guide to the Rulers of Imperial Rome, 31 BC–AD 476*. New York: Charles Scribner's Sons, 1985. Concise, but excellent biographies of all Roman rulers.

———, *The World of Rome*. New York: World Publishing, 1960. An excellent overview of the history and culture of Rome during its greatest period of influence (133 B.C.–A.D. 217) by a leading historian specializing in the ancient world.

Patrick Howarth, *Attila, King of the Huns: Man and Myth*. Carlisle, PA: John Kallman, 1994. Presents the history of Attila with quotes from primary sources. A separate section deals with the many different legends about Attila and the differing views of him in the Western, Germanic, and Hungarian traditions.

Harold Lamb, *Charlemagne: The Legend and the Man*. Garden City, NY: Doubleday, 1954. A detailed biography with many interpretations and conclusions by the author.

Paul Ratchnevsky, *Genghis Khan, His Life and Legacy*. Cambridge, MA: Blackwell Publishers, 1991. A thoroughly researched examination of Genghis Khan's life.

Mary Renault, *The Nature of Alexander*. New York: Pantheon Books, 1975. Mary Renault has written many books on Alexander. This one is a detailed examination of his personality rather than of his military and political accomplishments.

Henry T. Rowell, *Rome in the Augustan Age.* Tulsa: University of Oklahoma Press, 1962. Good for basic background material.

Chris Scarre, *Chronicle of the Roman Emperors, the Reign-by-Reign Record of the Rulers of Imperial Rome.* London: Thames & Hudson, 1995. Highly readable short biographies of all Roman emperors. Time lines, portraits, and comments by modern authors add to the interest.

Alan Schom, *Napoleon Bonaparte.* New York: HarperCollins, 1997. Over 900 pages, this work fully documents every aspect of Napoleon's life and career, but Schom's negative opinion of Napoleon is evident throughout.

Eugene Tarlé, *Bonaparte.* New York: Knight Publications, 1937. A full and detailed biography.

Steven Béla Vardy, *Attila.* New York: Chelsea House, 1991. A thoroughly researched book with many quotes from primary sources. Written for younger readers by a professor of history who specializes in eastern and central European history. Examines the life and times of Attila, king of the Huns, and discusses his image in myth and history.

Richard Winston, *Charlemagne.* New York: Harper & Row, 1968. A scholarly biography.

———, *Charlemagne: From Hammer to Cross.* New York: Random House, 1954. An earlier edition of the author's 1968 biography.

Periodicals

Adam T. Kessler, "Treasures from Inner Mongolia," *USA Today Magazine*, May 1994. An article mainly about the art exhibition that toured the United States in 1994; also contains some good historical information.

Internet Sources

Alexander of Macedon Temple. www.sangha.net/messengers/alex.htm. This site is put out by the Maitreya Sangha Society, a Buddhist group fostering the brotherhood of man. A tribute to Alexander; contains basic biographical information.

Attila website. http://art1.candor.com/barbarian/attila.htm#Hun. Good basic source with leads to other sites. The site is authored by Diether Etzel, who claims to be a descendant of Attila.

Charles the Great, King of the Franks and Emperor of the Holy Roman Empire. http://pages.prodigy.com/charlemagne. Good information here, plus many links to related sites.

Nina C. Coppolino, "Augustus." http://orb.rhodes.edu/encyclop/early/ De_Imp/auggie.html. A ten-page biography, the author's assessment, a list of annotated ancient sources, and a full bibliography.

Internet Medieval Sourcebook. www.fordham.edu/halsall/sbook1h. html#Charlemagne. Contains text of selected primary sources.

E. L. Knok, *History of Western Civilization*. Idaho: Boise State University. http://history.idbsu.edu/westciv/charles. Excellent site with specific information on different aspects of Charles and his times.

Nicolaus of Damascus, excerpts from *Life of Augustus*. Translated by Clayton M. Hall, 1923. www.csun.edu/~hcfll004/nicolaus. html. Tells who Nicolaus was and gives excerpts from his contemporary biography of Augustus.

John Popovic, *Alexander the Great,* Alexandros III Philippou Makedonon, Alexander III of Macedon (356–323 BCE). Project by John J. Popovic. www.1stmuse.com/frames. An excellent resource with much material gathered from several sources.

David Silverman, "Sources on Augustus." http://web.reed.edu/ academic/departments/classics/Augustus.html. An overview of various ancient sources on Augustus indicating aspects covered and providing an analysis of each ancient writer's bias. Contains excerpts from some sources as well as extensive commentary by Silverman.

Virgil, *Aeneid*. Book VI.ii. Internet Ancient History Sourcebook. www.fordham.edu/halsall/ancient/augustanencomions.html. Good basic source of Virgil. Includes excerpts from translations of his major works.

ADDITIONAL WORKS CONSULTED

Bullfinch's Mythology. Middlesex, England: Hamlyn, 1931.

John Canning, ed., *100 Great Kings, Queens, and Rulers of the World.* New York: Taplinger, 1967.

Anne Commire, ed., *Historic World Leaders.* 5 vols. Detroit: Gale Research, 1994.

Edward Gibbon, *The Decline and Fall of the Roman Empire.* One-volume abridgement of this eighteenth-century classic by D. M. Low. New York: Harcourt Brace, 1960.

Great Lives from History. Vol. 1. Pasadena, CA: Salem Press, 1998.

Mary Johnston, *Roman Life.* Glenville, IL: Scott, Foresman, 1957.

Harold Lamb, *Genghis Khan and the Mongol Horde.* Hamden, CT: Linnet Books, 1990.

McGraw-Hill Encyclopedia of World Biography. New York: McGraw-Hill, 1973.

Wess Roberts, *Leadership Secrets of Attila the Hun.* New York: Warner Books, 1985.

J. Kelley Sowards, ed., *Makers of the Western Tradition: Portraits from History.* Vol. 1. New York: St. Martin's Press, 1991.

INDEX

PICTURE CREDITS

ABOUT THE AUTHOR

Claire Price-Groff is the author of several books for young adults. She particularly enjoys writing about history and the people who made it. She lives in the mountains of western North Carolina with her husband and their little black dog and orange marmalade cat.